The Zen of Glass Shard Painting

An Introduction to a New Art Form and

An Exploration of Personal and Artistic Development

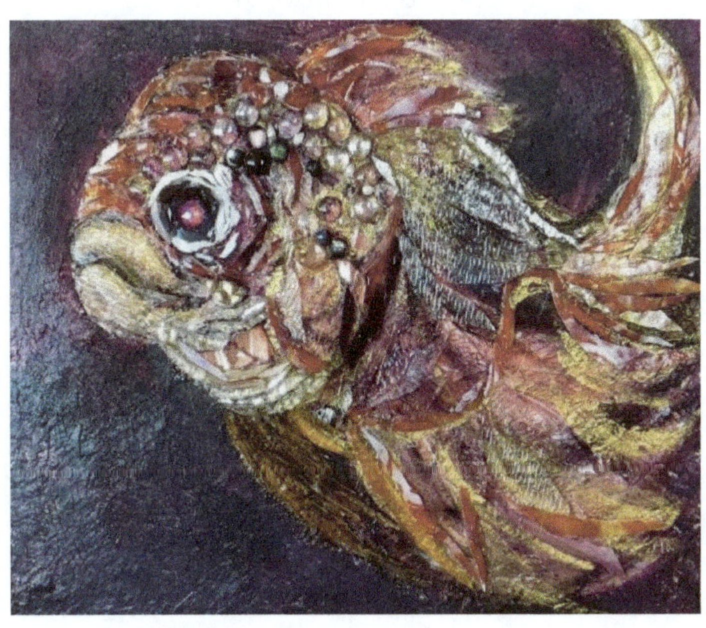

Dr. Eleanor Ruth Fisher, PsyD

ISBN: 978-1-962849-95-1

Dedication

All of this is possible because of the love, support, encouragement, criticism, and partnership of my husband Dennis who is the essence of the eternal namaste.

Acknowledgements

I must acknowledge the Marblehead Art Association as I receive unlimited encouragement and support in continuing the development of my Glass Shard Art.

I also acknowledge all those whom I have met on my journey. You have motivated me to keep going.

Table of Contents

Dedication ii

Acknowledgements iii

Chapter One: My Journey, The Beginning 1

Chapter Two: Motivation, Creativity, and Positive Disintegration ... 9

Chapter Three: Developing a New Art Form 16

Chapter Four: My Studio and The GSP Process 34

Chapter Five: Selected Works, and Their Conceptual Development
.... 41

Chapter Six: My Gallery, and Portfolio Samples 86

Chapter One: My Journey, The Beginning

October 3, 1991 is my 're-birth-day'. Nineteen ninety-one did not begin happily. Frightening and strange events appeared, slowly at first, then daily, including losing letters in my speech and having difficulty standing up. My words disappeared in the middle of a sentence. After a few seconds, I would continue to speak normally. This happened two days later, and then three days later and then, the following week. The frequency was increasing, and significant other symptoms were developing.

Subsequently, my pronunciation lost its clarity. I remember saying, 'if I don't emphasize my D's, I'll lose them'. Then thinking, where did that come from? My attempted solution was seeing thoughts, sentences, and words in my mind before saying them out loud. The solution did not work.

Next began the diminishment of motor skills. To rise, I placed my hands on the arms of a chair, my feet almost shoulder width, then pushed myself up; weeding in my garden, found me lying on my stomach, the only position available to me. When I attempted to bend over or kneel, I collapsed. With some free time, as I tried to play golf, I pushed my golf trolley and managed to finish the first hole, then feeling faint, had to leave.

After consultations with three neurosurgeons, each expressing a casual wait and see attitude, I was referred to Dr. Ojeman at Mass General Hospital in Boston. Reviewing the tests of former neurosurgeons and listening to my symptoms, he showed me an x-ray of my brain which was projected on a screen.

As we looked at the tumor, situated at the bottom right rear quadrant of my skull, Dr. Ojeman told me I had a meningioma, a commonly slow-growing tumor whose cause is not well understood, yet they often do not cause noticeable symptoms.

Consulting him in September, showed that the tumor had grown to be as large as a lemon at the base of my brain. He closed his hand into a fist which approximated the size of the tumor.

Explaining its growth and probable etiology, he added that a brain tumor can begin to grow pre-birth; however, based upon my history, most likely it had been growing slowly since I was a child."

This was followed by his statement, "surgery was an immediacy." Two weeks later found me admitted to the hospital and prepared for brain surgery the following day.

The preoperative information I received, and lifetime memories caused by the growth of the meningioma were so traumatic that until recently I could not remember its name. Meningioma is considered unusual and rarely cancerous, with about 20,000 cases a year reported in the United States.

The key was in my hand, finally clarifying why a great deal of my developmental behavior had been so uneven and bewildering. Many agonizing years passed trying to understand myself without success. The idea of a brain tumor never occurred to me. All the while it was there and growing and my ability to accomplish tasks which needed logical thinking were diminishing.

Not only did Dr. Ojeman remove my life-threatening brain tumor, but he also explained to me how it affected my development and behavior. Listening to him was the beginning of understanding the disconnection and loss of myself, my innocence, and the accompanying overwhelming shame and countless life altering experiences I had created and endured without knowing why. As he spoke, I sobbed, starting to mourn the anguish filled years caused by my ignorance of the tumor and its impact on my entire life.

The left-brain functions which were affected by the tumor included limits on language (for me, learning foreign languages), math, and science. Math, up to and including fractions had been easy. In elementary school my father tutored me in these basics every evening. Advanced math and their concepts, on the other hand, were beyond me. Logic and analytical functions had been limited since I was a child.

No matter how I tried to think of a way to fit in with the other kids, I could not. To make matters worse, I learned to read in kindergarten when I was three years old and consequently entered public school with a double promotion. It was supposed to be a reward. It was not. It was an 11-year sentence and an invitation to mock the youngest student, a gifted bewildered girl with asymmetrical development.

The meningioma grew slowly. Certain brain functions were not possible, such as considering consequences beyond immediate gratification including thoughts about long-term results. On the plus side, specific things such as reading and comprehension far beyond my grade level, memorizing my lines for plays, and being on time were not difficult for me.

I could make decisions and was quick to understand tasks related to other brain functions, quickly learning what not to attempt such as subjects involving science, foreign languages, and math beyond fractions.

The right hemisphere of my brain functions had always been available to me. The tasks of the right hemisphere compensated for the continuing growth of the brain tumor in the left hemisphere. The right brain functions include art awareness, creativity, insight, holistic thought, music, awareness, 3d forms and left-hand control imagination, intuition.

The right hemisphere functions enabled me to make good decisions based upon education, experience, and intuition. I was able to build and keep a busy full time private practice for 40 years.

As was my custom, mid-March of 2020 found me in the garden clearing the debris of winter, home to the critters who lived and hibernated outside. The soil had become friable, and it was time for spring cleaning and planting the earliest greens.

My being overflowed with gratitude. Without brain surgery I would have died. I heard from my spirit guides, saying, "you did the best you could, the left hemisphere of your brain was not available to you for most of your life."

At that moment, a flash of understanding occurred. It was electrifying! My book of life opened, slowly and in minute detail. I read each page. Everyone was present, as usual regurgitating all their banal defenses. Each rationalization was well-rehearsed and often used.

I forgave myself instantly, owned my behavior, while fear and past suffering along with its immediacy mostly evaporated.

The journey towards becoming an artist and personality integration began during surgery with an out of body experience. It was composed of two parts. My parents appeared to me; they were very happy and holding hands, wearing their best clothes, enjoying a family celebration. They told me, "The time to join us is not now, you have much work to do, we love you and will guide you."

Secondly, while immersed in a warm, fragrant bath, its water colored like a rainbow. I heard, "This is the font of compassion; with this new understanding you will enter and become part of a different dimension. The price of entry is that you will learn to paint."

"Eleanor, you're OK," were the first words I heard when Dr. Ojeman gently awakened me from anesthesia. "Now I can learn anything," was my first thought.

Other disintegrations began about a month later. Several alternatives would flood my mind at once; my thought process became multifaceted, resulting in confusion. My personal life was stagnant, still, surrounded with negativity and tolerating emotional abuse.

"Get it fast, don't procrastinate, that's self-flagellation" I told myself. I knew the time would come when I'd crash and burn. I didn't know how long it would take to dynamite myself from hurtful behavior and blow the entire structure to smithereens. For years I suffered from post-traumatic stress syndrome.

Another benefit from brain surgery and integrating at a higher level came with the introduction to my spiritual self. Previously, I had no knowledge of the inner journey as it related to the development of spirituality and compassion. The spiritual journey is filled with action, each step firmly balances on actualization and morals, values, and standards.

On a beautiful, early spring morning, standing before a blank canvas, pencil in one hand, the other holding my T-square, I froze. Appearing on the canvas was the phrase, "your journey." Instantly, the shadow disappeared; realization dawned; my thoughts and feelings of being healed were goals.

Returning to my office and patients about 3 weeks after brain surgery was a wonderful experience. Feeling more alive and healthier than I can remember, I was eager to be with my patients again. My recovery was speedy, and I was driving my car and playing golf by the end of the month. None of the symptoms I had with the tumor have ever returned.

Shortly after returning to my office, while talking to a patient, I glanced to the left, towards a side window, the size of a tv small screen. "What happened," she asked me, I responded, "oh nothing, just a small cramp in my neck.". That was not true. It was as if an invisible hand gave my head a push to the side. In a fast-forward instant a complete film of her life appeared and been projected onto that window.

Unbeknownst to me, my spirit guides were introducing themselves. After she left, I felt shaken, terrified that my brain tumor was returning. It was not returning. Instead, it signaled hearing the word, 'paint', for 6 weeks, once daily, at random times. Finally, I was convinced it would not stop unless I painted.

Going to a local art store, I asked for the six biggest canvases they had, the largest easel, stumbled through thinking aloud and asking about how to paint with oils, how they were used and what and if they were mixed with anything. Then, I asked the clerk to give me whatever oil paints or palette knives needed along with pencils, erasers, mixing instructions and anything else since I was going to teach myself to paint.

I heard the familiar voice saying, "Have faith and remember." My spirit guides reminded me that the price I agreed to pay for complete health was learning to paint and they would guide me". "Okay," I said, "I'm ready. I will begin as soon as I get home."

The information I received from the clerk in the art store was about my first and only art lesson. It never occurred to me that I would need a teacher.

My garden and the ocean top the list for first inspiring my artwork. A butterfly appears whose wings have colors of orange, yellow, black, and gold. Using photos of my garden, and all who live here, I copied several sections taken at various times of the day trying to create what I saw. After many sketches, something that seemed to resemble my garden began to appear on the canvas in front of me. I began mixing and applying oil paint using the colors from my photos as my guide.

Time stopped; my work merged with my garden and time as I moved to another plane. Visualizing the oceanic experience in utero, I am the unborn baby. Like my unborn baby, I am enveloped in silence, attuned only to feelings. We are nestled and nurtured in the womb, preparing for life. There are calm, and steady heartbeats and the squawking protests at the insult of birth.

The window in my studio frames the ocean. As I see the incoming and outgoing tides, hearing the sea with their myriad life cycles, I feel a sense of wonder. A lifetime is inadequate to capture this; the inspiration is infinite.

The experience of beginning to draw and paint was irresistible and profound. New knowledge included sketching and painting, both literally and in my mind, observing my fingers touching textures and smelling bouquets from petals and leaves which were not there. What was occurring was cognition, the "mental action process of acquiring knowledge and understanding through experience and the senses." My curiosity and emotions were generating new knowledge. Each time I sketch or paint I am learning. GSP has become one of my passions and my life has grown exponentially.

Understanding the development of cognition continued when a completely unexpected event occurred. During a continuing education class at Boston University, whose focus was study of the brain, the instructor showed a picture and asked if there was anyone who could name any colors.

Everyone said "Grey," except me. Asked to describe what I saw in the picture; I responded that the dominant color scheme is turquoise. "Soft turquoise like the walls in my bathroom," and I finished, saying, "There are shades of orange used as accents."

After class, I asked the instructor to tell me why I was the only one who had seen the colors I saw and if she thought that having brain surgery had anything to do with it. She responded saying, "Sometimes when there is a traumatic experience to the brain this sort of phenomena may occur; the name of this condition is synesthesia". This explanation helped me begin understanding the major changes which had and would occur.

I was completely unprepared for the new changes. Teaching myself to paint was and is an astonishing experience. The colors were significantly more vibrant and appeared to have a new depth, dimension, and vibrancy. Along with this, I thought I saw more colors and shades than were on a paint chart I was using. Fear of being laughed at and told my imagination was working overtime meant that I did not share this information with anyone.

Synesthesia is a perceptual phenomenon in which stimulation of one sensory or cognitive pathway leads to automatic, involuntary experiences in a second sensory or cognitive pathway. Not a lot is known about how it occurs, and there are variations which may cross over.

Observing myself, I became convinced that synesthesia has many dimensions and is individualistic. We have heard about musicians for whom the notes seem to fly off the page and authors whose characters tell them what to say. They have their own form of synesthesia which is intrinsic to their creativity.

Synesthesia enables me to see and paint color combinations which have appeared in my dreams. The glass shard pieces have a voice and guide me as to placement on the canvas. I hear, "Put this shard on that one over there, use that, then put that one there to create shadows." Guidance continues as I hear, "Start another layer over there and use those other colors not what you have in your hand."

When I make mistakes, there is no hesitation in removing entire sections until finally the right colors, and elements have come together.

For me GSP's are both an emotional and physical experience where nothing else exists. Carving and placing glass shards, sometimes smaller than ¼ of an inch is very intense and concentrated causing me to work two to three hours at a time then take a break. I listen and observe allowing the work to evolve.

When each GSP comes to life, I hear, 'I am complete.' Then I know I have done my best.

Ideas of a predictable life, controlling the familiar and unfamiliar no longer exist for me. Merging with an unknown side of my developing creativity brought me to a new world where nothing was familiar or predictable.

Newly perceived emotional stimulation develops with each sketch and painting. This process deepens and expands my senses and are expressed in my paintings.

The GSP's are multidimensional and glow with their layers of glass; each has their unique story and invites you to connect with them. My desire is that each time you see them you feel refreshed and eager to revisit these other worlds and lives which exist beyond the physical.

I love to see people stand transfixed as they first see the GSP's. When they buy them for their homes, I am thrilled. They now own a piece of infinity which has come through my hands, directed by the timeless masters. Each piece is created with my entire heart and soul. The owners feel this, and often we have become friends.

My life is full of passion, excitement, challenge, bleeding fingers, burns and scars. It is all that I have ever wanted. As was my custom, mid-March of 2020 found me in the garden clearing the debris of winter, home to the critters who lived and hibernated outside. The soil had become friable, and it was time for spring cleaning and planting the earliest greens.

All of this is possible because of the love, support, encouragement, criticism, and partnership of my husband Dennis who is the essence of the eternal namaste.

Chapter Two: Motivation, Creativity, and Positive Disintegration

A major purpose of this book is to address the longing of people to live while expressing their creativity as a total human being rather than exist in a state of fragmentation. Searing questions involving personal meaning in life with accompanying ambivalence can cause untold anguish. Facing these issues by answering these questions requires motivation and introspection. Desperation accompanied by anxiety, depression, and unending dissatisfaction will often be the motivation to consider doing something different. Simply stated then, "Enough dissatisfaction makes motivation."

Those who are motivated to be creative as a way of life must become passionately dedicated to its development to see it through. This usually happens only after having explored ways of fitting in, doing it the "right way" and learning that this sort of compromise leads to disconnection from oneself. For others, the ones who do not fall into the "socially correct behavior" trap, find sufficient motivation to move forward in a positive, healing way.

Another important factor in the complex calculus about motivation is the psychological basis behind the sometimes-difficult decision to choose a life of creativity.

When I was about fifty, I was introduced to The Theory of Positive Disintegration (TPD) written by Dr. Kazimierz Dabrowski. Positive Disintegration under Dabrowski's theory means restructuring the underlying organization of affective and cognitive functions. It is called "disintegration" because the lower level of functioning must break down before it is replaced by a new organization of a higher level. The term positive is used in the same sense as when we speak of evolution from lower to higher forms of life. Rather than in terms of age or learning, development is measured in terms of structural and functional reorganizations. By this definition if there is no restructuring there is no development. Positive development is associated with positive disintegration.

This theory is a monumental, groundbreaking work through which gifted children and adults can be identified including the levels of their giftedness, characteristics, and accompanying behaviors. For me, TPD was mesmerizing. I could not put Dabrowski's book down. The work was like oxygen to me, and I was dying. For the first time there seemed to be answers to why my life evolved as it had, why there were so many crises and conflicts. One thing stood out for me - I had never known that I was gifted. Why was I so emotional, took things so seriously, felt so deeply and differently, "overreacted" compared to others? I learned I was fragmented and different, trying to cope by isolating myself. The only comments I heard as a child were how smart I was, leaving me with the idea that being smart was what mattered. Reading TPD, I began to learn who I was for the *first* time in my life, what my behavior meant, and that I was not a freak to be mocked. There were others like me! Tears began streaming down my face. Then, I heard sobbing. It was me. There were others to talk to, they would understand. It would be a first for me. As I continued reading, each line of the three-page preface spoke to me. The process of my development was discussed, and I understood it for what it was.

Seeing that my life had been full of conflicts, anxiety, sadness, and depression I read that these feelings are called dynamics; an integral part of positive conflicts which are essential to the growth of personality and creativity. These experiences caused me to develop coping skills which would help me survive. I learned this was an example of "accelerated development" and that these wrenching experiences were necessary to promote my overall personality growth and development.

As a child, I remember my principal family dynamic was "Don't upset your mother" but mostly my childhood was made up of my parents and grandparents who took care of me before I went to public school. My memories are all about being happy, playing with the neighborhood kids, reading books, friends, and Friday night sabbath lighting the candles, putting money in the charity box before we ate chicken soup and challah and roasted chicken - and I got the wishbone!

I have introduced TPD in this book because it gives people a tool with which to examine self-motivation and creativity. TPD emphasizes recognition of the unique genetic developmental potential of everyone. Dabrowski states that the strongest developmental genetics will find expression regardless of the environment, in some cases, by overcoming the environment or even by transforming it. In 1977 Dabrowski and Piechowski authored a paper about artists and creativity. The theory offered a framework for examining components and the dynamics of giftedness and creativity. Dabrowski named heightened capacities of those people he studied who possessed, "intensity and richness of thought and feeling, vividness of imagination, moral and emotional sensitivity of those who are creative and strive for perfection". Their interactions with the world of subjective experience seemed to be over and above the common and average in intensity, duration, and frequency of occurrence.

Dabrowski saw this behavior as indicating strong *developmental potential* and named them "forms of psychic overexcitability". Dabrowski stated that one of the critical principles for understanding developmental potential is the presence of overexcitability in response to stimulation. When this occurs, an opportunity is created for the person to dis-integrate their biological and social conditioning and to re-integrate a structure and system of consciously chosen views of self and values. This creates intense experiences, leading to conflict and crises between the person and their social roles. (Dabrowski et al., 1970)

Dabrowski identified five forms of overexcitability: sensual, psychomotor, emotional, imaginational, and intellectual. He believed that some individuals may show potential to develop beyond biological impulses and social norms. If present, this potential is expressed through a consistent pattern of over-reaction to both external and internal stimuli. His work concerning developmental potential illustrates the ability to be self-reflective where the focus is knowing the difference between what is and what ought to be and *attempting to live what ought to be*. That has become my focus!

When present, overexcitability changes a person's view of life, as one "Sees reality in a different, stronger and more multi-sided manner." This causes a person to come into collision with many things, persons and events and creates a wider and more intense experience of reality.   Dabrowski states, "In this sense, overexcitability is a "tragic gift", contributing both positive and negative features: positive in that one is now able to fully appreciate the wonders of life; negative in that overexcitability causes human suffering, injustice, and sorrow. Overexcitability creates conflicts and anxiety that necessitate the search for personal meaning, fuels disintegration and leads to advanced development. Emotional overexcitability is at the heart of advanced developmental processes, and if present with imaginational and intellectual forms, they give rich possibilities of development and creativity."

Communication involves listening, hearing, and responding and my dad always listened and responded to me. If he had a question, he asked me. When I asked him a question, he was always patient and explained things, math for example. In the fourth grade it was hard for me to grasp fractions. My dad taught me how, and when I turned in my homework, my teacher didn't believe I did it. I showed her I had learned fractions. It never occurred to my dad that there were people who would be cruel to me; not believe me.

The first night after reading about 30 pages of TPD, while dreaming, I heard myself saying, "There *are* others like me." Scenes from my public-school years followed, two years younger than my classmates, showing me shunned, and humiliated. I kept repeating, there are others like me. I am not alone.

Continuing to read TPD was fascinating, and I realized that understanding this was a key to my development, both personality development and creative development. As I read case studies followed by detailed descriptions, I recognized myself and knew that TPD was a map leading me from fear into the discovery of my authentic self. I didn't know how, just that I would begin.

Familiar, repetitive issues came to mind. I needed to go deep carrying a large flashlight, wearing huge boots. I would slog through the muck. I needed to understand how to grow into a total personality. Fear needed to be left behind or become my closest companion. I didn't want to be afraid anymore. I heard, "You learned to paint; you have begun to create; there is enough time." I wanted to believe that my life had a purpose. My intention became, 'I will, I can.' Throughout my life, the question, 'Do I have enough strength to get through this? came to mind. Enough strength was available; the voice of Creation led me, although I did not know its name. With the aid of the TPD theory, I began to analyze who I was and how much my history determined my present life. With a flash of insight, I knew I could create a different present, future, and history, barely understanding how much I needed to learn.

Stumbling across the phrase, "You are the author of your life," was like bolts of electricity shooting into my core. "Everything? Yes, of course, everything", my mirror assured me. At that moment, I decided to write my life story worthy of a Pulitzer Prize. The earlier chapters were full of sadness and pain. Those memories stand as a reminder of being broken, split in two.

I think it's important for us to examine what I see as the practical uses of Dr. Dabrowski's TPD. In the following paragraphs I have provided examples of the overexcitabilities Dabrowski theorized to make them relevant to what I am writing here. These overexcitabilities can be thought of as filters through which both internal and external information can be processed. Understanding of course that for each of us the filters may be partially open, closed or seem nonexistent, and of course different for everyone.

Sensual Overexcitability: Since my artwork includes mixed media, textures are a given, ranging from glass to fabric, pieces of jewelry, to rocks and seashells of all sorts. These are irresistible; while looking at them, even briefly, my fingers move as if I'm touching them. Sometimes, it seems as if that gorgeous black sequin blouse wants me to touch and feel its essence. I acknowledge its beauty. The purpose of each object reveals itself, often differing from my first ideas. Thoughts of using any object always bring new ideas and possibilities.

Psychomotor Overexcitability: This involves feeling very excited at the thought of creating a new piece of art. Rarely do I think of one piece at a time, instead, many ideas come to mind at once and I know I need to calm myself down, so I can think clearly.

Emotional Overexcitability: This includes my relationship with each painting and the elements involved, whether a person or animal. I think about the subject, their milieu, and their story. While designing clothes, creating a setting, or painting flowers, the details must be authentic and right for them within the specific work. I don't want to disappoint the soul of the GSP; I am responsible for the story's accuracy. TPD states that the conflict in development is always between "what is" and "what ought to be. This is mainly a function of the power of emotional overexcitability. The famous American philosopher William James said, "The intense experience of emotional overexcitability can cause a person to constantly feel challenged to action, which effects their entire life".

Imaginational Overexcitability: I often describe myself as living with one foot on earth and the other tap dancing in fantastic stories, plays and movies. Stimulation for these come unbidden; full of images, smells, objects inviting me to touch them. I have to slow myself down or I become overstimulated and cause myself to be confused. This applies to my dreams as well, and my husband often hears me talking in my sleep as if I'm going to school, telling my teachers, yes, yes, I can do that or uh-huh.

Intellectual Overexcitability: My middle names are "why" and "learn". I want to know why and how to bring life to each GSP. This goes beyond curiosity; the questions continue in my dreams. I love to observe. While in my office with patients or supervising other therapists, I have always spoken of being an observer seeking to understand, intellectually, spiritually, emotionally, and physically.

Another purpose of this book is to cultivate awareness on the part of the readers about the creative process. Telling the stories includes those teaching myself to paint. My desire is to create an emotional communication bond between myself as the artist and you as the reader. It also allows a more sensitive awareness to various aspects of your feelings as I speak to that creative part of you which hears, sees, and feels.

The experience of art is completely emotional, or it is not an experience, it is a critique looking for flaws. I think it's important to note that there are seven common elements in art. These are: line, shape, texture, form, space, color, and value, and they are all used singly or together to help the artist communicate their work. These elements bring harmony and help to organize any work of art and they also present a constant challenge. They must be used efficiently and in such a way as to complement each other, not conflict with each other. Using glass in art does not change any of that, just makes it a bit more complicated as it adds another element and dimension.

Many of you readers who are artists or engaged in other creative experiences have been formally trained. I have had no training in painting and have learned through copying the 'masters' and attempting to understand the stories told in each painting; as well as the various paint and brush techniques they used to bring their stories to life on canvas.

My method is to study and continue to understand people, the magic of color, tell my anecdotes, and develop my style. This is often bewildering, yet at the same time always challenging and exciting.

I attempt to understand the feelings expressed in the paintings of other artists, textures used, various elements and nuances. Initially, exploring the artist's intentions, causes me to feel incompetent, never having known or thought about their motivation or point of view.

Learning to paint begins with thinking of my lesson today. My questions include what the artist is saying, and formulating questions about the colors, techniques and what makes this picture real? How do I feel looking at it and why?

"Oh well", I say, remembering I was a lifelong student, followed by, "Give yourself a break, you are learning."

Chapter Three: Developing a New Art Form

Jason Aronson, M.D. wrote in 1964 that the Theory of Positive Disintegration is outside the current modes of personality theory: therefore, a "brand-new theory". My book is in part about the process of the development of the art form I have named Glass Shard Painting. Since GSP is also outside the current modes of art, according to Dr. Aronson's definition, it is therefore, a brand-new "theory".

This book is also a study of a woman whose creativity and personality have been developing since birth – *me*! My growth has been chaotic, often undecipherable; at times tremendous highs were experienced, followed by unexpected, ego-shattering lows The lows felt like Dante's Inferno at the ninth circle; "What happened, what did I do wrong, how do I get out of the torture of this hell?"

Silence.

Growing up as an only child with codependent parents meant that for the most part they left me alone. My father did tell me two things which shaped my life: "Don't upset your mother, get a good education and you can do anything you want in life, Princess;" his name for me.

I heard my father's words telling me not to upset my mother as a warning; do not complain, or cry or get mad. Being told not to upset my mother frightened me and created a life- long need to heal people and, attracted me to those whose lives were endlessly problematic. It should come as no surprise then that I was like a magnet attracting manipulative people in personal relationships. When I felt rejected, or heard raised voices, whether in a social or personal situation, I became silent, afraid of what I had done wrong. The little girl inside me did not understand what was happening and felt guilty and punished. This was a repetition compulsion. All of this resulted in me becoming a psychotherapist, a healer. I could not help to heal my mother, but I can help to heal others.

Despite her chronic depression, my mother was the model of a productive businesswoman. She was a successful buyer of high-end women's clothes in an upscale Boston department store. Dressed in beautiful clothes for work, she exuded confidence. She looked wonderful, like a fashion magazine cover. She taught me how to dress and use accessories, jewelry, and makeup. It was a great mask. When she was home, she was depressed and always wore old house dresses. She suffered from bipolar disorder; today's medications were not available and shock therapy was used to try to alleviate her depression.

With that family history as prologue, I can more clearly outline my transformation into an artist. This journey is one that evokes the origins of personal change through creativity.

I am honored to be named after Eleanor Roosevelt, a brilliant woman whose creativity changed the world for the better. In 1933 Eleanor Roosevelt was forty-eight years old. She was asked how she transformed in her life as she aged. She answered, "Little by little." Then added, "As my life developed, I faced each problem as it came along. As my activities and work broadened and reached out, I never tried to shirk. I never tried to evade an issue." Reading about her transformation and suffering inspired me to commit to my own transformation -- little by little.

Artists often hear the beat of their own drummers, along with feelings of alienation, depression, and desperation. It is among the gifts leading to personality transformation offered to all artists.

The birth of glass shard painting began with my first bewildering efforts at learning to create them on a spring morning after awakening from a lucid dream conversing with my spirit teachers. (Lucid dreaming and interpretation are common to me since a major part of my professional training has included dream analysis.)

Before sleeping, I thank my spirit guides and ask them to guide me in my artwork. During lucid dreaming, I am often aware of the conversations and my participation in them. In the morning, my husband would say, "I heard you talking last night." "Well," I respond, "That's right. I was having my art lessons. Did you hear what I was saying?" He repeated what he heard me say in my sleep, "No," "Yes," "Aha," "Yes, I can do it," "I can do that." I tell him, "Sounds like what I remember." The specific dreams about my art lessons may be forgotten, yet there is no hesitation as I begin to sketch and paint. It's like my teacher is right there, guiding me and what I'm doing is easier than I expected.

In May 2013, while dreaming, I was introduced to a concept far beyond anything I could ever imagine. My guides informed me that, "Since you began your journey as an artist, your lessons, learning to sketch, paint in oil and acrylics were successful. Now it is time to learn something brand-new.". The last brief comment I remember was, "Go smash glass. We will guide you."

Hearing this, tears began to roll down my cheeks, awakening my husband. When I told Dennis what happened he was his usual supportive self, saying he would help me and not to be afraid. Going downstairs for breakfast, all my paintings seemed to say, "Me first, me, me, me." Where to begin? And how? On the kitchen counter was a clean green wine bottle I had washed, ready for recycling, and I thought I guess that's where I'm going to begin.

Dennis appeared carrying a heavy metal mallet in one hand and a flat paving stone in the other, saying, you can break glass with these. Wrapping the green bottle in a dish towel, I smashed the glass against the cinder block with the mallet, at the same time wondering, "Now what do I do?" Initially, I collected many colored wine bottles and continued smashing them in the same way. I eventually expanded my search for glass to include various glass plates and serving pieces from a local shop and then to a warehouse with thousands of sheets of marvelous glass, of all colors and textures, that stained glass hobby people went to.

The next challenge was in fixing the glass pieces and shards to the canvas. I tried various fixatives looking for something that would quickly and solidly adhere glass to a vertical painted canvas, finally settling on hot glue. It was easy to apply, dried quickly, and was strong enough to hold anything I was likely to want to apply to my canvases.

For all my GSP I paint the picture first and I use the painted picture as my template for applying glass shards. With hot glue the glass shards can be placed to conform to the painting or slightly off kilter if that suits me better and several layers are often used to create a 3-D effect that is real and inviting.

Each session creating glass shards brought lessons, most of them unexpected. One of my first lessons was how to apply hot glue so that my fingers would not be burned. What was the correct amount so the glue would not leak out the side of each shard, yet have a secure hold? Eventually, I learned about finger covers which allowed me to press the shards into place without my fingers getting burned by the still very hot glue, and still allow me to "feel" the pieces I was adding to the work.

Each night I go to sleep thanking my spirit guides and asking for guidance. One of my first questions to my guides was, "Why I was not told about using the hot glue gun so I would not get burned?" The response was, "You didn't think before you used it; you always learn the hard way." It seemed obvious they thought they had a sense of humor.

In my personal library is a beautiful book illustrating the work of Mary Cassatt. There was a particular painting having many elements that I knew could teach me a great deal if I were to try to copy it. I asked my guides how to proceed. The response, "Just paint what you see, you can do it." This is not what I was looking for. I awoke feeling very frustrated and as soon as I was able, I went to my studio and began my first attempt. The painting provided me with wonderful lessons. I entitled it 'Learning to See'. The subject was two women drinking tea. The dress of one woman was a many-shaded, plaid, iridescent silk dress. Another woman sat rigidly, and, wearing yellow gloves, was raising her teacup to her lips. They looked away from one another. The tension between them was papabile. In front of them sat a table with a silver tray and tea set. The silver and its reflections, and the cups and saucers sparkled and shone.

I set up my canvas, propped open the book, and said a little prayer asking Mary Cassatt to guide me. My concentration was complete as I tried to hear what she was saying. The picture was a Victorian vignette of two rigidly polite, controlled, verbally silent women having tea. It felt as if this was the first time I truly saw the Cassatt painting. One aspect was an iridescent sleeve next to a silver tea set. I knew I must learn to paint an old silver tea set, an iridescent streak on a sleeve and a yellow gloved hand holding a teacup. Clearly these were difficult but "must learn" things for me. Seeing became multidimensional, including my eyes, my senses and twitching fingers wanting to feel all the textures. I was able to "get" the silk taffeta iridescent fabric and various textures while capturing the tension between the two women.

Attempting to recreate the colors and textures, I chose shades I thought could be blended to produce those I saw in the original. As I applied the colors, I heard, "That's fine," or, "Mix a little white in with that blue." Other times, I heard, "No, that is enough, do not overpaint, it's messy, be patient. You are doing OK, you are learning."

My intention was to learn despite the difficulty I suspected all new artists must endure if they are to get better. On entering my studio. I always said, "There are no mistakes or screw ups, just learning and to have faith, not fear". Then I began. Often, I heard pieces of directions which were given very quickly, as if they were speaking to an advanced artist with many years of experience. I asked them to slow down and to remember I was just a beginner. The usual response, "you will catch up, there is a lot for you to learn." Eventually I heard them more clearly and was better able to follow the directions. The Mary Cassatt painting lesson turned out well. Today this painting hangs in my studio. It reminds me to always return to the basics. I repeat this constantly: learn and listen to what *they* tell you. Keep it simple, allow the painting to tell its story, see the shadows and nuances cast by the shards, be coherent. If it's not right, remove the glass and do it again. Each GSP is unfinished until I hear its voice telling me that, "We are alive and complete". When you have faith, fear does not exist. Welcome to my world and my journey.

I never visualized myself as a passionate artist. As I was growing up, the word passion was always associated with romantic songs danced to and sung. But as I grew in my craft, I came to love being in my studio. It is a passionate eternal love affair. Passion has a life of its own which knows no fear and has no other choice. That is all there is. Passion is the fuel which keeps me going as I continue to listen carefully to the story told by each GSP. This is my life with my art. Before that feeling of passion arrived, I was frustrated and anxious to find "Real Art", whatever that was. It was like there was a huge jagged missing piece. Its name was art. It gnawed at me, taunting me to find it. There were too many lessons yet to learn. The passion and release of merging with art was unavailable at that time. I was miserable. I was ready when I was ready. It is what it is. It is not what it is not.

When I had 'glassified' about ten paintings of the more than 100 that I had completed it was time to get opinions of several significant people in the art world. I felt the need to have some professional evaluation so I could be sure I was on the right track and not wasting my time. Even though my husband and friends thought the GSP's were worthwhile, it was important for me to hear from some art experts whether continuing to develop them was of any value.

Dennis called someone he knew and as a result, appointments were made with three experts in the art world to visit my home and studio.

Before they came, Dennis asked me what I would do if the opinions were that my work was not salable. Without hesitation, I replied, "nothing different, I'd feel bad for a couple of days, then I would keep doing it. I want to get better, more elegant and refined and eventually the world will catch up with me, hopefully, while I'm still alive with all my marbles intact."

Two of the three people who came to see my work were educators at a local art college, and the third was director of a well-known art association. All three were enthusiastic about my work, agreeing that they had never seen anything like it and urged me to keep on working. Except for being away for brief amounts of time, I have worked in my studio almost every day since.

My struggles and fears mirror those of others; 'my paintings are ridiculous, what I am trying to do is impossible, laughable, and arrogant'. All this was underscored by feelings of gross inadequacy; who am I to want each painting to be alive, tell you their story causing your soul to feel refreshed? How can my work encourage the development of anyone's unique creativity?

During my dreams I heard Dr. Dabrowski telling me, "Do not be afraid to paint. Conflicts are essential for you to learn higher values and morals."

I also heard the voice of Dr. Abraham Maslow talking about naïve creativeness which Dr. Dabrowski felt was resourcefulness and imaginativeness in the service of beauty and other needs.

When hearing criticism or comparisons, I would inquire, "What makes you say that?" Previously, I would be speechless in the presence of criticism, fearful of the censure I was sure would follow. The need for safety is at the base of fears. How does quaking silence create safety? Having learned to recognize when I was beginning to slip into a place loaded with negative emotional messages, I say, "I'm not going there, the price is too high." Understanding that re-watching the movie of my childhood and adult fears is a choice, I choose not to go there. How does reliving all that help? Finally, 'getting' this, I take my fears with me and continue the development of GSPs.

When I realized I was asking for approval of my work, (which meant that I was asking approval of myself), other questions occurred; how much approval would I need, and for what? If I had approval, what would that mean? Whose approval? Would approval guarantee complete love and acceptance? Whenever I began to lose confidence, I reminded myself that the approval I needed was in my mirror and the reflection saying, "I do my best, what more is there?"

Giving up my spontaneity and creativity was not an option. With that understanding, invisible weights I had carried for years lifted. At that time, I discovered a piece written by Maryann Williams. Her wisdom is boundless as is my gratitude and respect for her. "Our worst fear is not that we are inadequate, our deepest fear is that we are powerful beyond measure. It is not our light, not our darkness that most frightens us. We ask ourselves, "Who am I to be brilliant, gorgeous, talented, and fabulous?" Who are you not to be? You are a child of God; you're playing small does not serve the world. There is nothing enlightened about shrinking so that other people will not feel insecure around you. We were born to make manifest the glory of God within us. It is not just for some of us, it is in everyone. And as we let our own light shine, we unconsciously give other people permission to do the same. As we are liberated from our own fear, our presence automatically liberates others."

As the development of GSP proceeded, my goal to become an integrated personality continued. I knew no other life was acceptable.

As I chronicle my experiences, I listen to my spirit guides whether asleep or awake, I respond saying, "Yes, I can, yes, I can do that." This has become the foundation of my philosophy of life.

People think about their legacies as they get older. If I could leave a legacy, it would be, "Dear reader, every day you will hear yourself say, "Yes, I can, yes, I can do that, I will have faith, not fear." Please join me, as I birth my work. I know that no matter the mess the paintings look at times, their unique story will be told.

My years of training as a psychotherapist focused on the importance of emotional communication, the primary tool of healing. For me, emotional communication is instinctive and for all my GSPs my most important tool is my compass rose, naming each feeling as the work takes shape, the direction it's going and its emerging story.

Emotional communication is what I consider my eighth element of art, assisting the other seven in the story which appears on the canvas. What am I leaving out? What do I want to keep hidden? Why?

When feeling lost, I default to emotional communication, asking familiar questions. If it's not right, without hesitation, layers of shards are removed, the canvas repainted, if necessary, wash and recut new glass. Begin again. I listen and follow; the elements lead me as well as the soul of each GSP.

I am a phenomenologist, a storyteller, delighting in telling stories, using gestures, intonations, dramatic pauses and voices that I hear. This is the why and how of GSP. Of course, I can't use gestures or facial expression or tone of voice to communicate via my GSP, so I have come up with alternatives in my glass shard art. Each piece tells its own story with a beginning, middle and end. All of them issue an invitation to enter a world beyond dreams where all is safe, and you return refreshed, eager to explore, again and again. Here are some examples of what I mean by that.

Self-Identification

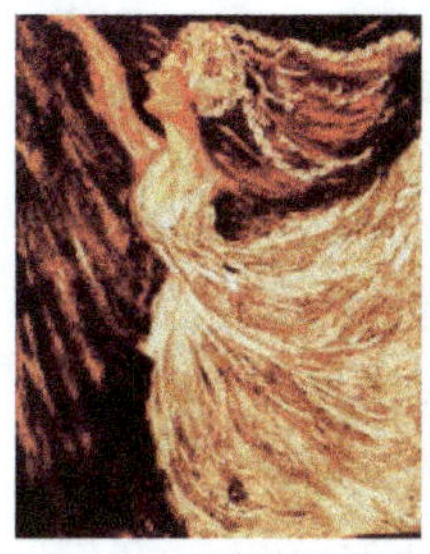 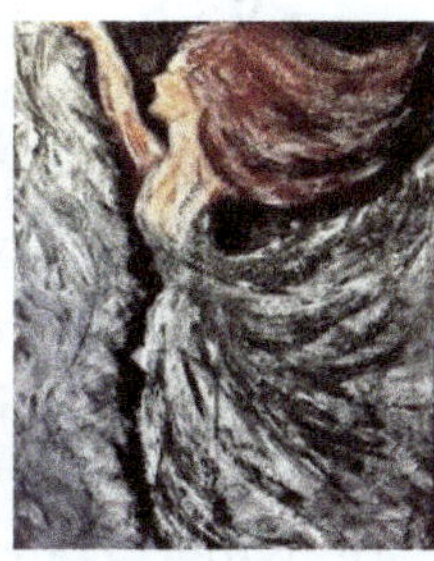

This is the name of a story in the first GSP at left whose theme is the multifaceted dimensions of women. She is far from ordinary; her eyes and mind see here and there, almost simultaneously. Her passion is limitless; intelligence creates thought followed by another idea, and how, why, when. She flies, adorned in a dress of pearls and diamonds, her hair streaming like the ends of a kite. She is limitless. She is woman. This second image shows the initial painting before she claims her birthright of vibrancy and color while still in the time of mostly black, white, and gray. Nevertheless, she knows about the joy of her colors and their expansion into her rainbow. She will, and does, pick the perfect time and colors.

The Play

Examples of my creative process are important to include here. One of my goals is to create a believable story with each GSP. I want to create one in which you keep looking, and indeed, cannot stop looking. My GSP I call "The Play" provides a good example of this.

The following pictures show the process I used in developing a glass shard painting with a specific subject and goal. Step one is mentally writing a paragraph describing the elements in the story, providing an important guiding template.

After deciding what sort of story it will tell, I fit a name to it. The name of this is "The Play" because it evokes the subject, albeit from two perspectives. Could it be a play with the characters in position on the stage, or is it really a view of the audience, watching the play, each character showing some different reactions. The setting is an Art Deco nightclub which was in fashion from around 1910 through 1939. I wanted to emphasize a sleek and anti-traditional elegance that symbolized wealth and sophistication. Also emphasized were curved lines, colors, and fashions of the day.

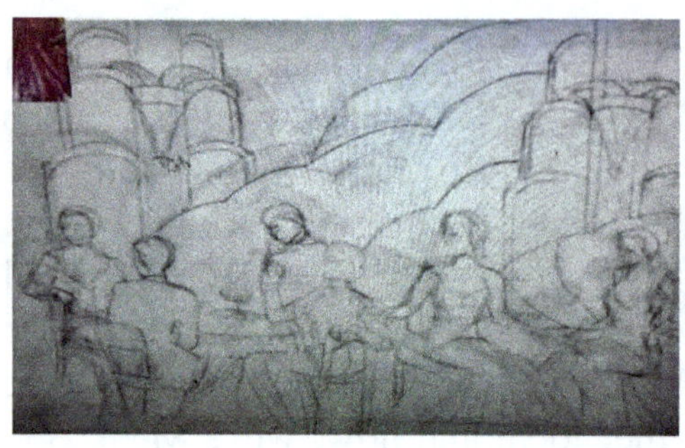

With my research completed, I began sketching unhesitatingly, directly on the canvas as if I were copying a picture sitting next to me. My goal is always to lightly pencil in a preliminary sketch. Using drawing curves, a soft relaxing background for the nightclub began to take shape. After the walls and their curves were clearly delineated, framed windows and mirrors were added to complete the picture that supported the story and goal.

Since in this era a nightclub would likely have sconces for some of its lighting, I looked for convex glass in my supplies and was able to locate the colors and shapes in a candy dish I no longer used; handily repurposed into glass shards!

The question of the number of people who would make an

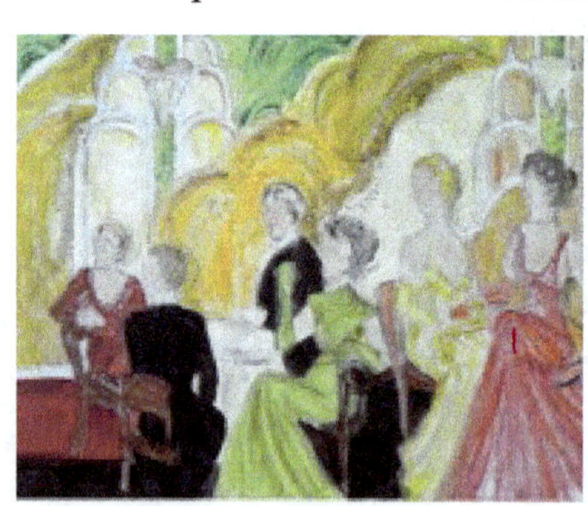

interesting story and its subplots brought forth in my mind the number five. After the initial sketches I first began a preliminary painting, simultaneously visualizing the emerging scene as if I am one of the characters and from the perspective of the audience/observer. As I painted, I began to design Art Deco clothes, deciding on popular colors, and added common furniture for the era to yield a believable scene. The clothes, hair, jewelry, and accessories all contributed to the overall impression of the time and place I had in mind. My intention was to create each figure with a different personality, fully present in their behavior and dressed for the occasion. At this point in the development of the piece I may add or subtract something, all the while observing to ensure what I am painting brings the story to life.

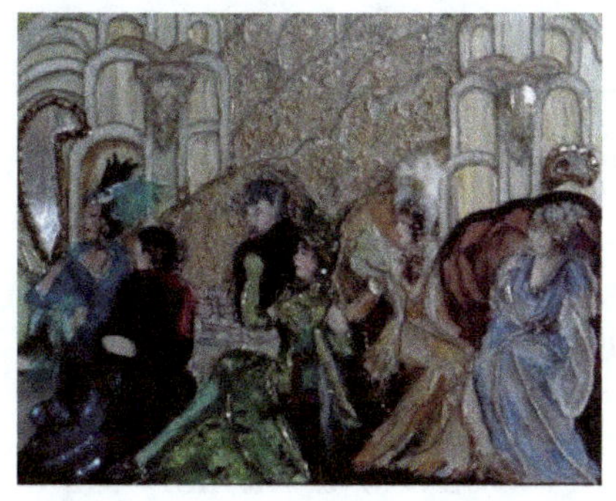

Inherent in many of my pieces is humor, as I think of life with a touch of whimsy adds a positive addition to the entire work. As I mentioned above, the title, "The Play," derives from my intention to have the viewer decide whether the people you see are characters in a play or watching the play. What do you see?

A Deux

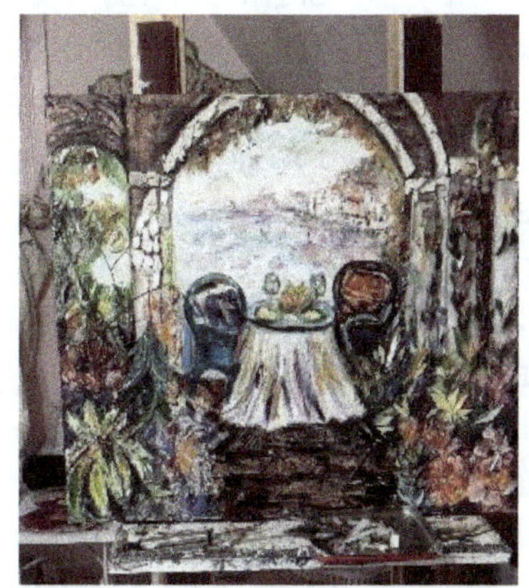

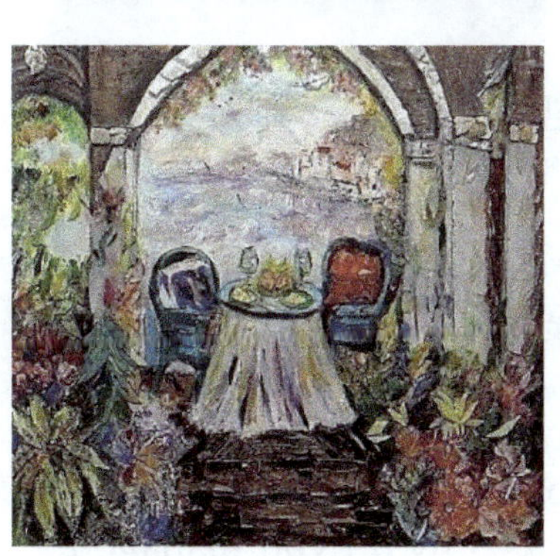

There are always challenges and questions as I begin to formulate a specific GSP. The first image at left shows the almost completed painting in my studio. This is a challenging time as each detail must be checked, singularly, and then as they affect the entirety. This image presents the questions to be asked before beginning the finishing process. For example, do the flowers have enough leaves and highlights, how do I finish the bottom of the tablecloth, is the bower of grapes over the table and chairs plentiful or are more grapes and leaves needed, what time of day or evening would be best? The list of questions goes on and on in my mind. I don't have a checklist since all my GSP are different, with completely different questions as to the details and how they integrate to tell the story.

Taking photographs of the sessions provides an additional perspective, almost as if another person was pointing out things that I had not seen.

The first photo was taken in a dim light, and the one below it was taken with a brighter light. I was amazed to see what appeared to be two different pictures with two different moods based upon the lighting.

Depending upon the light source, the completed picture below represents a view of a subdued romantic evening or breakfast or lunch for two on the patio.

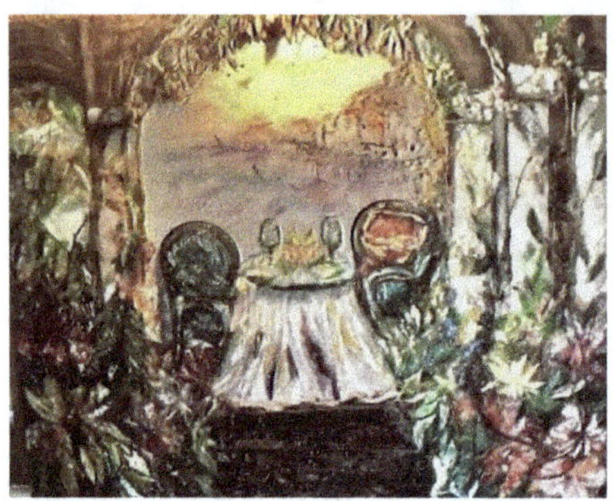

A Deux is a memory of a never-to-be-forgotten experience at four o'clock one afternoon. My husband and I were exhausted from a day of sight-seeing and came across this nook at our hotel on the Amalfi coast. Sitting down underneath this bower of hanging grapes, surrounded by flowers, we ordered a favorite bottle of wine, fruit, and the region's famous, delectable buffalo mozzarella cheese, made fresh every morning. Naturally it all had to be topped off with an espresso and some limoncello! The view and the cool breeze from the sea created an extraordinary moment of perfection. I took many photos as I knew I wanted to share this memory later.

<u>Aquarium</u>

The painting Aquarium is from my series of Life and Gardens

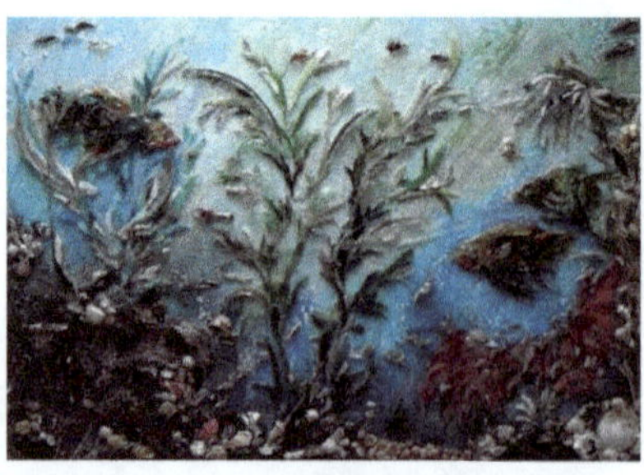

Under the Sea. When people see the paintings in this series, they are full of questions; "How long did it take you to do this? Where did you get your glass? How do you manage to get all these things on canvas?" I love answering them and showing them my studio and my special wet-saws and my special nippers, glue gun, etc.

Aquarium is another good example of a GSP that illustrates my technique. Aquarium has a sand-textured base, intermingled with sea grasses, stones, and shells. The fish swimming around have been carved from Murano glass brought back from a visit to Venice, Italy and Murano, Italy, where exquisite glass is created. Each piece of glass, seashell and stone presents a challenge in cutting and carving and placement so that the unique lines and colors in every piece are visible.

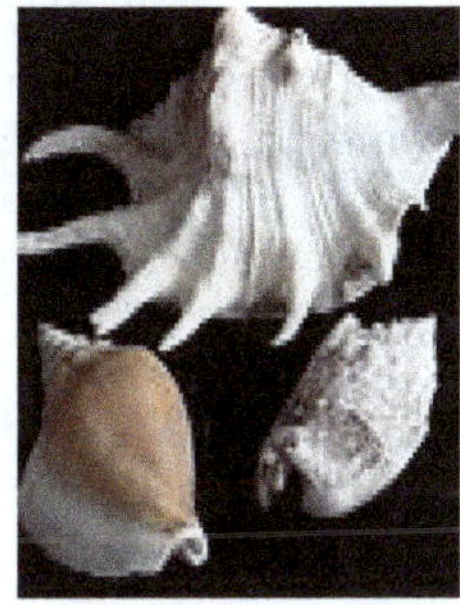
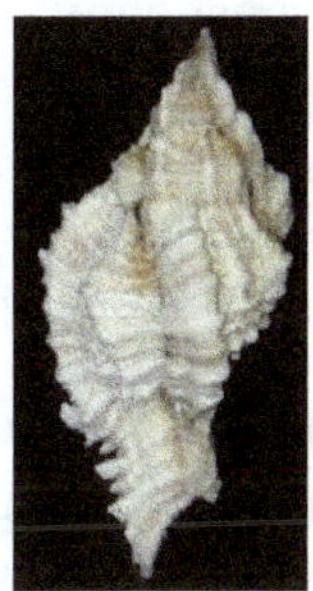

The photo above on the left shows a shell with sharp finger-like protuberances. This is a part of a large strobilae for my "garden under the sea". All seashells I like to use help to create the flora and fauna which is visible throughout this GSP. One of my favorite varieties of shells is the apple murex. Its shell is thin enough for my midsize saw blade to cut through the ridges easily and cleanly.

Apple murexes are mostly tan or light brown with darker brown markings and white highlights. This is helpful since I use a lot of earth tones in my work. The shell is thick, and the surface is rough. The aperture is glossy and either white, tan, or peach. Its ridges lend themselves to designs which blend easily with the reefs and sea life, rock

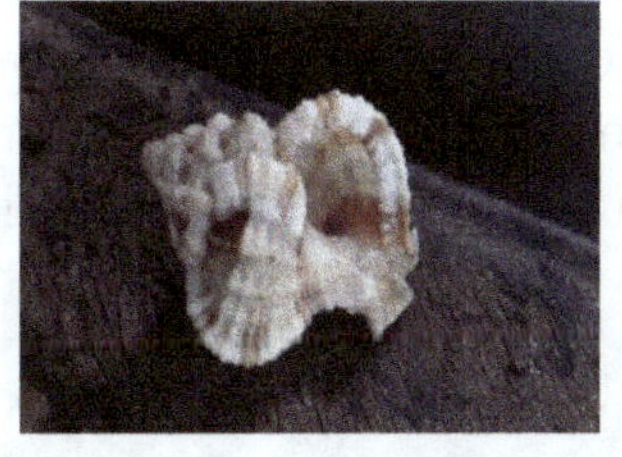

developments, crannies, and homes for fish and flora of all sorts. Many of the seashells I use are large and thick. Maintaining the uniqueness of each shell necessitates carefully maneuvering a shell into position, as I slowly cut through the ribs of a beautiful, reddish apple murex seashell or a conch. Slicing through these beautiful shells provides many opportunities to create diverse examples of life under the sea. These photos show only a fraction of the great variety in shape and color of the shells I use.

<u>Outside My Window</u>

This is one of my first paintings. The first book which I wrote, Beyond the White Light, contained the story of going to the art store and asking for the six largest canvases they had, the largest easel, how to paint with oils and what equipment was needed. I was determined to fulfill my obligation and agreement made with my spirit guides before waking from brain surgery. I heard, "you will be all right. However, the price you will pay is that you will learn to paint."

Outside My Window was one of the six huge original canvases I bought in 1991, following brain surgery. In 1992 the canvas was hung on the wall where I first drew it, then painted it with oils, mostly using pallet knives. The painting of the mural was completed after much work in 1995 as each painting session was a lesson, as I continued to learn how to paint.

Eight years later, in 2013 when my guides informed me in my dream that I had learned enough and could now smash glass, all my 100 finished pieces flooded my mind, and I had no idea of where to begin. I thought of the mural 'outside my window' and knew that it was too large to bring up to my studio to cut and apply glass shards. I asked my guides how to do this. No answer. Then, realizing it was way too much for me to attempt at that time, I stopped, knowing that eventually I would complete it.

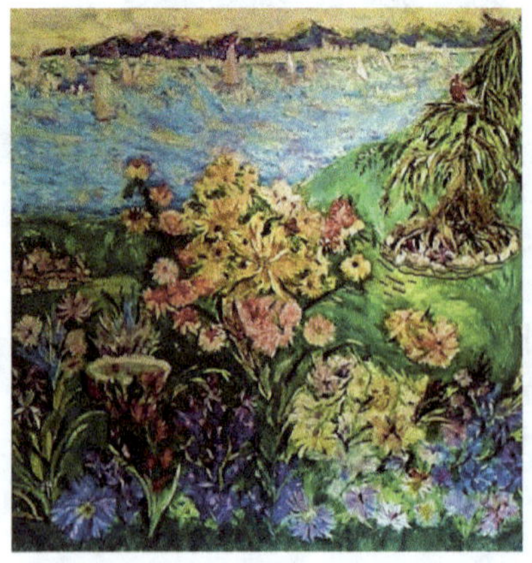

It was not until 2018 that I dreamt of how to do it, and heard, "it is time to finish this, "you have learned enough, you will be able to 'glassify,' it while still on the wall.

The process began by removing the small amount of glass which had been applied earlier.

Before I began selecting glass for the mural and considering other elements I stood back, and several questions and issues came to mind. The flowers were not swaying in the gentle breeze from the sea. How could I bring this vignette to life? What would cause me to feel invited to walk in this garden? How do I hear Nahant beckoning from across the bay?

It was quickly obvious that the entire mural needed to be cleaned, and several areas repainted, including the ocean, sky, reflections, trees, and some foreground. I had gained a great deal of experience as a painter since I had done this piece and now was the time to put those new skills to work.

What follows is a sample of self-talk as I studied the many elements of this GSP: "There is a large bird bath surrounded by flowers at the bottom left. The water is not sparkling, shimmering, or calling to the thirsty cardinals, blue jays, and squirrels this morning", I was eager to receive this information when I slept.

Before I go to sleep, I ask for specific help. Because I'm an analyst, I watch myself analyzing my dreams as I sleep. My dreams are always in color, making it possible for me to see accurately what I'm being told.

The next morning, I covered the pool table which is located directly in front of the mural and on it I spread previously carved glass shards, containers with various colors of glass, my hand glass nipper and glue gun. I also placed my 6-foot ladder at the side where I would be climbing up and down for the next 8 months.

As I worked on the left lower quadrant containing the birdbath and its flowers it began to feel alive; the cardinal calling its mate, the creatures who live in the garden and the shimmering, dancing water.

The town of Nahant glowed with the noontime sun on its sandy iridescent shores, and I was sure that I saw my friends waving to me from across the bay. Finishing this first session after about six hours, I stepped back, astonished.

Eventually, after about 8 months, thinking I could do no more, I heard, "I am complete." There may be a bit more to do, such as finishing the boats that race from Swampscott to Nahant. However, when I asked people's opinions. They say it's perfect, Leave it alone.

Outside My Window is dedicated to my husband, whose encouragement and love is reflected in every shard.

The sea is my companion and source of constant inspiration. Often it mirrors my experiences, with its highs and lows, debris in and then swept out, rusty sewer pipes which leak then get fixed. The sea is home to boat races, surfers, and the myriads of people with and without their boats, kites, balls, and dogs which come and go.

Outside My Window is the childhood creation of my dream of having a beautiful garden by the sea. Amongst my childhood memories, I recall that my father always brought my mother and me gladiolas. They became my favorites, especially those tall yellow and bright orange ones whose petals glowed like the wings of butterflies.

When I was 10 years old, I wanted a garden. A tiny patch of dry ground sat in front of my home. My father handed me a tool, saying, "give it a try, but I don't think the ground is soft enough". After briefly attempting to pierce the merciless, unyielding dirt, I realized it was impossible. That disappointing experience caused my dreams of having a garden resulted in the notion being put on a backburner with my vow that someday, "I will have a beautiful garden with lots of mirrors and fairies will live there with me."

When I bought my present home in 1981, its history included that of a well-known, prize-winning gardener. She was the first owner. I was third.

The garden I had promised myself as a child began to emerge a few years after I bought this house. It was the beginning of an ongoing love affair with my garden. First on my list for a garden was a tall white wooden fence encasing the entire property. It would not be possible to create my magical garden by the sea without these boundaries. A local garden designer created the bones of the garden which included two levels. The planting of the sections began with several large anchor trees, a semicircle of low evergreens to mark areas and an island off center with soft curving lines flowed, inviting eyes to move from one interesting area to another.

Buying an entire set of garden encyclopedias from the Brooklyn Botanical Gardens, I began to learn about what would grow here and why. This was augmented by my library of garden books which I kept buying, eventually filling up six large shelves of others garden wisdom. Soon after this research began, while considering what to add each year, I knew my garden needed a name. Garden by the Sea was my first thought. It was perfect. To celebrate the birth of my long-awaited garden, I painted a door sign for the outside of the garden which included cardinals, robins, butterflies, and vines. The garden gate spoke to me, and I painted a large fairy queen who sits high on a branch in a blossoming Appletree wearing jewelry with butterflies accompanying her on adjacent panels. This was the inspiration for the GSP, Fairy Flower, my alter ego.

The garden has always been my sacred space for healing and meditation. Each year, March 15 heralds the beginning of cleaning and preparing my garden, first removing the protective debris from last fall which had nurtured many animals over the winter and added much needed mulch for the soil. Next, the soil is readied for the nurturing of the perennials and the new babies who will grow and flourish here. The work continues daily for about two months, as I eagerly await the first peas and string beans planted in the sunniest protected area by the house foundation.

Can you imagine being pregnant with several babies and the accompanying feelings? I liken this to a sonogram which is used to monitor and evaluate the progress of pregnancy. For me this equates to imagining each GSP as a fetus growing moment by moment, waiting to be born. All details are continuously reviewed, and changed and added, then carefully noted. Guided by our focus, the process is trusted and followed.

Labor before birth is unimaginably painful, bloody, messy, a miraculous happening and completely awe inspiring. Eventually, the moment of birth is imminent. I am overcome by excitement, having heard the voice of every glass shard guiding me to, "do this or that", so that each contains their unique characteristics.

The instructions from my guides have been followed exactly. Voila! Done. Each one emerges saying, "I am complete". My gratitude is limitless.

We have done our best; their story has been told and when they come to you their destiny has been fulfilled. Each has the same purpose, to present you with a reminder of eternal beauty.

The opportunity to contemplate a moment of perfection, asking nothing in return, is yours.

Chapter Four: My Studio and The GSP Process

My home studio with its high ceiling and bright light pouring in makes a wonderful workspace. There is plenty of shelving for my equipment and supplies plus abundant closet space for canvases of all

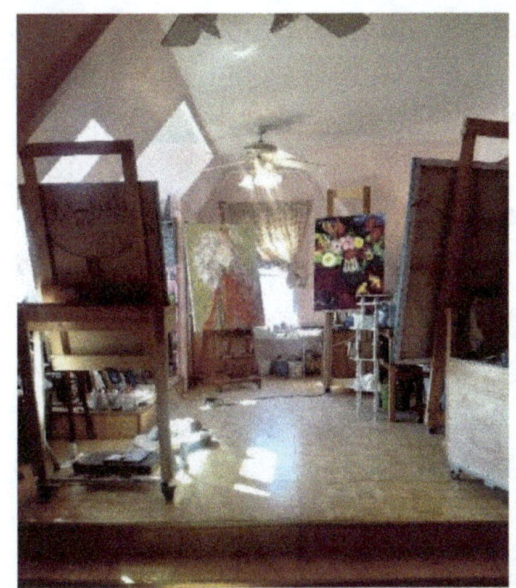

sizes. I am relaxed here as nothing exists for me except complete focus on the task at hand. The work is intense. As discussed earlier, I must first visualize my desired image then sketch and paint it in acrylics. Then and only then can I begin the process of applying the glass shards. The glass I want to use must be carefully selected then each shard must be cut and carved first with a special diamond-bladed wet-saw, next shaped by hand with glass nippers and then precisely placed on the canvas with hot glue. I use a lot of colored glass and I'm lucky to have friends who check with me before they discard decorative pieces, knowing I may be able to use them in my art.

What follows is the how-to part, or how I create my glass shard paintings, step-by-step, with some techniques in minute detail.

On the frame of the door to the studio are symbols of people sending love in many forms. Other talismans rest on the windowsill, which faces the ocean. My inner voice hears, "you are art in process."

Automatically, my left hand reaches for the eyeglasses waiting on a shelf at the entrance to my studio. If I'm using my saws right away, I also grab the rubber gloves. Creativity and safety merge comfortably here; shortcuts do not work. Among the first questions visitors ask me is, 'Where do you get your glass," or, "Do you paint the glass to get those colors, or "Do you pick up the glass on the beach"?

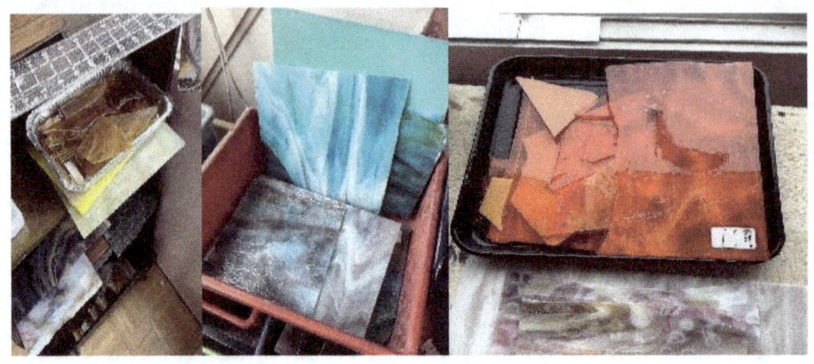

My answer is that I buy most of my glass from a glass wholesaler's warehouse filled with beautiful glass panes of every color and texture. Often both sides are different and complementary, an important element which assures that each GSP is a unique creation. Given all the variables, not even I can exactly duplicate any GSP.

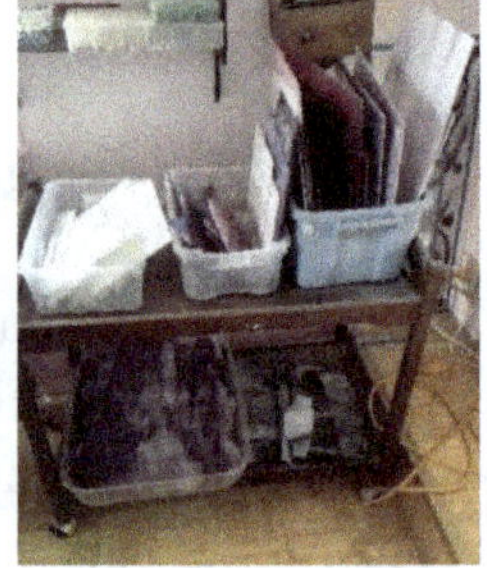

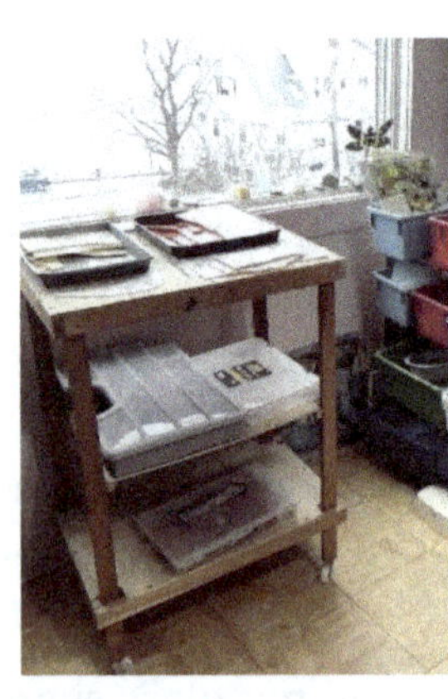

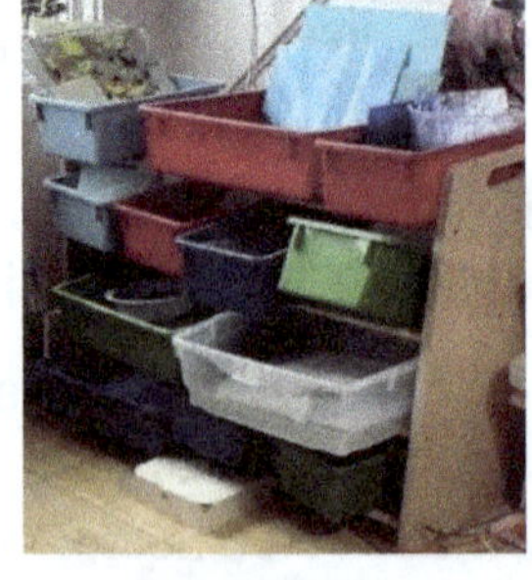

One corner of the studio overlooks my garden and the ocean, among my greatest sources of inspiration. The shelves on all sides of the studio hold distinct colors of glass categorized as to the shades and hues. Directly in front of the window is a table which my husband made for

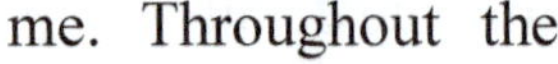

me. Throughout the studio, he has made all the shelves, tables and three of the five easels. What is distinct about this is that the tables all have wheels. Additionally, the easels have adjustable levels that allow me to use any size canvas.

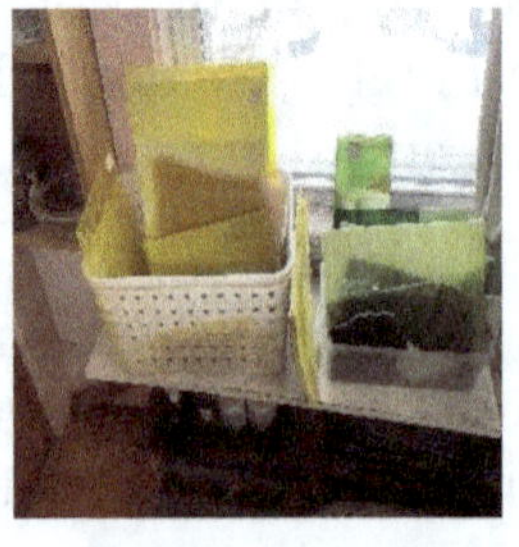

The following photos show some additional samples of glass; 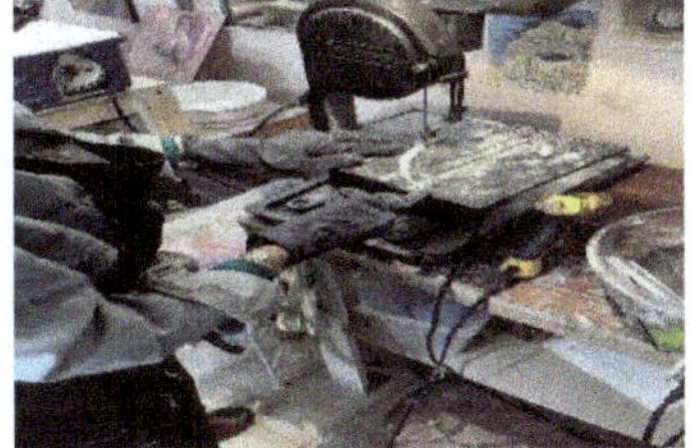 most of them have textures and patterns, while the reverse side has complementary colors and patterns.

I currently have three diamond-bladed wet-saws of different configuration, giving me the flexibility to choose the right tool for the task at hand. I have over the years used every glass-cutting wet saw on the market. None of them seems to have been made to last through the many hours over many days and weeks I demand. They either fail to cut well, leak water over the parquet floor of my studio, or the belt breaks or the blade breaks or other such issue that Dennis deals with as the resident mechanic.

For most cuts I prefer the band saw as it provides so many cutting 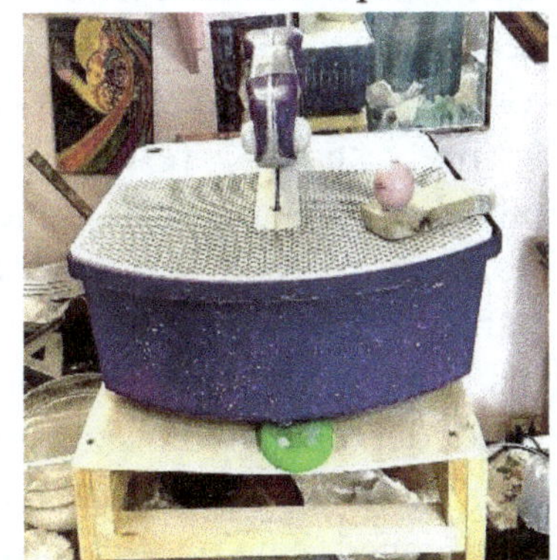 options. My ring saw is for the curvier cuts I want to make. The tile saw is large and powerful which I use for stones, marble, or bricks as needed. In the smaller saws the glass can be turned to make various shapes such as broad edges on leaves or to carve automobile fenders in a backward "S" shape. The primary word here is "feed" the glass into the blade; do not push. One feeds the glass carefully and slowly, otherwise pushing it against the blade can cause the blade to break. The two photographs at left show the beginning of cutting a curve. Always using rubber gloves, I guide the piece of glass using my "pusher," which my husband made for me because it was too difficult to feed the glass using only my fingers encased in rubber gloves. Pushing against a sharp piece of glass to feed it through the blade is not advisable! The pusher is placed at the front end of the saw prior to turning the saw on. The glass piece is then shaped by feeding it through the blade along the lines I have in my mind. Holding my hand on top of the pusher handle (cleverly made by Dennis using a golf ball), I guide the pusher forward against the glass, into the desired size and shape of the shard. I stand on a large wooden box sometimes to look down upon the saw for a better view of the cutting. The wet band saw can cut glass into very thin, long, and curved shapes without breakage. The photo above shows me carving a semicircle whose diameter is less than a quarter of an inch wide. You must be especially careful of the fine cuts as the slightest pressure in the wrong direction can cause the piece to break. There is no scrap glass as each piece is used. I love finding the piece I need from a broken bottle, for instance. If I want to shape the shard into a leaf, I make a rough cut with a saw then use my nippers to get the final shape I am looking for. By snipping the shard on both sides, I can create a stronger sense of reality. This illustration shows glass bits shaped to serve as a flower petal. The top is wider than the bottom and each end has a point where it will complement

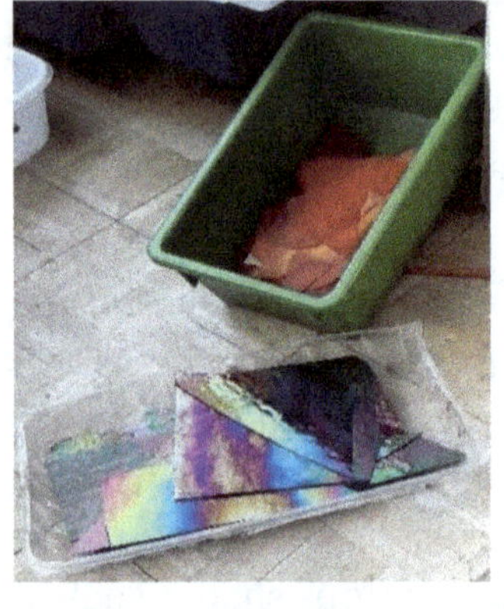

another leaf or petal and fit in easily to a design. Carving all the glass in a curve shape is basic to the GSP coming to life. For it to live and speak to you, each shard must be created in this manner. Plants are not made of glass, after all, and for this medium to work I must create a sense of reality with my shards resembling whatever nature has created. To create dimension, life, energy, and movement, every glass shard piece is carved, usually curved and always with pointed ends. This is done with my handheld glass nipper. How many snips I need to make depends on the size and purpose of the piece. After carving and shaping, each shard is individually washed and dried before being placed. The photos show me snipping a glass shard, which is then used as part of a leaf. They may be used for other designs, cut smaller or with ruffles as shown.

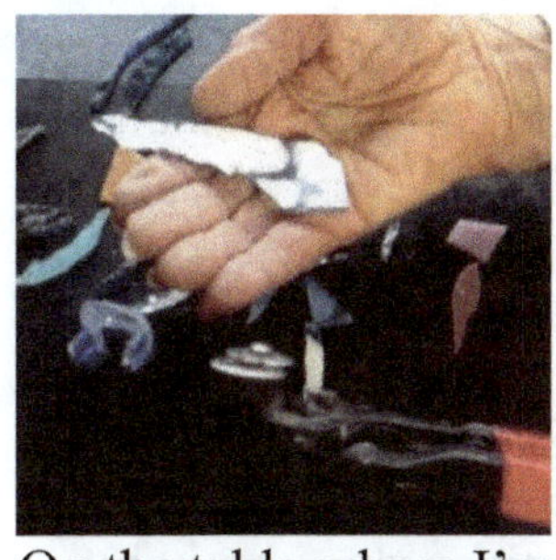
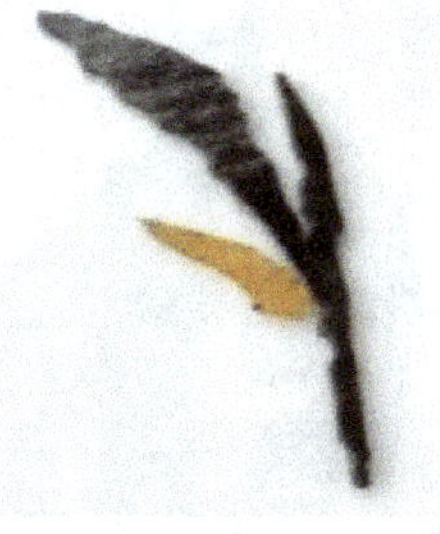
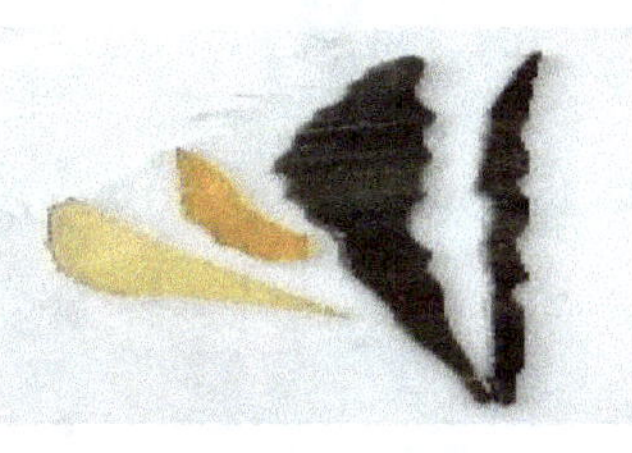

On the table where I'm using my glass nippers, are shards which have already been shaped from scraps.

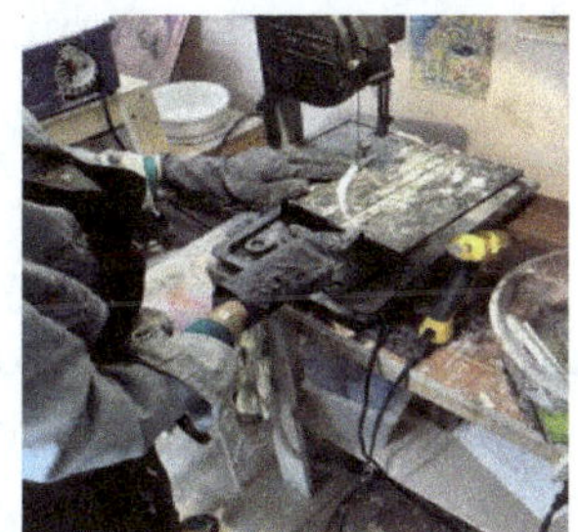

I am grateful that my studio is large and comfortable with plenty of light, including the dormer window overlooking the ocean in my garden. Inside, are views showing several easels and paintings in process. If I am preparing for a show, I may work on 4-5 GSP's at a time, checking if a shard is suitable for more than one piece. The five easels stand with work in various stages of development. Often several pieces are in progress at a time, allowing me to move from one easel to another, searching for the perfect placement for a shard. This photo shows me moving one of my easels. My husband put wheels on

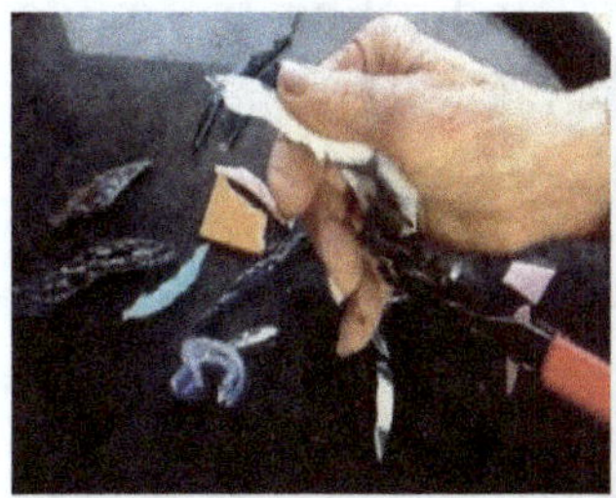
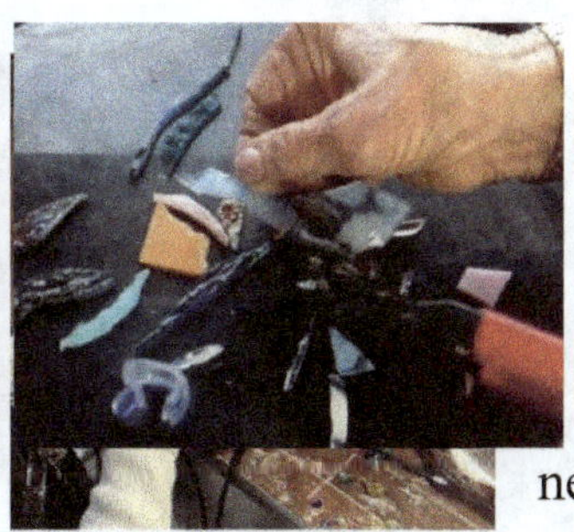

all of them. This is necessary as the layers of shards, stones and other elements cause the canvases to be heavy making it hard to move them, taking advantage of the light or to simply moving out of the way. Two easels have electric outlets on them for the glue gun and the heat gun. The easels also allow for multiple angles and the ability to be laid flat. Some GSP's are so intricate that removal of extra hot glue is needed before more shards are added. This can only be done with the heat gun

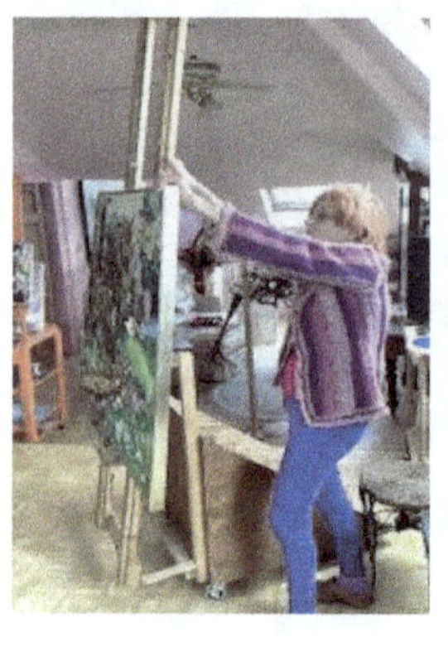
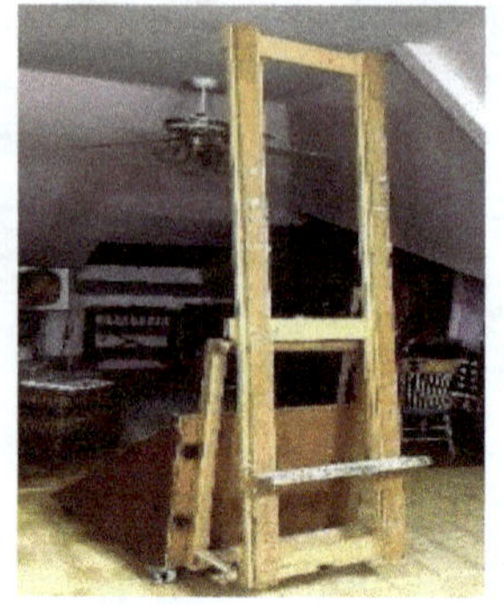

when the easel is flat. Other equipment includes band aids, first aid cream, and rubber gloves!

In creating an acrylic background that has texture, such as a starlit, nighttime sky, the paint is mixed with thickener, then applied with palate knives, using swirling strokes. With the wet and uneven background, sprinkling with iridescent white dust, finishes this process. I also mix sand of different grits into the paint when I want to add that sort of texture.

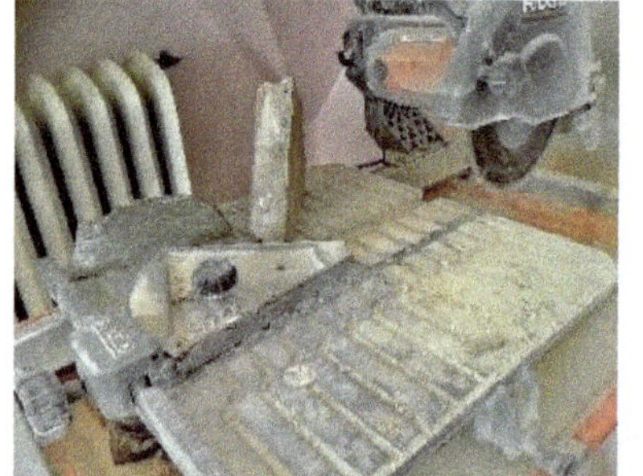

At left is the previously mentioned diamond-bladed saw used for heavy-duty work with both stone and glass. It has a pump to keep the blade wet while cutting through marble, stone, tile, and glass. The blade can cut angles of any degree by adjusting the guide.

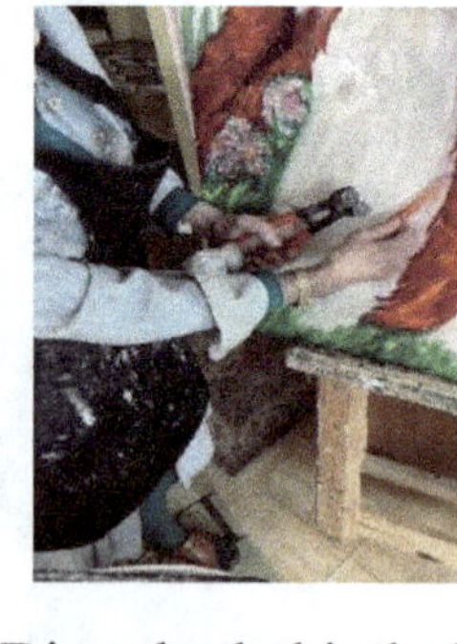
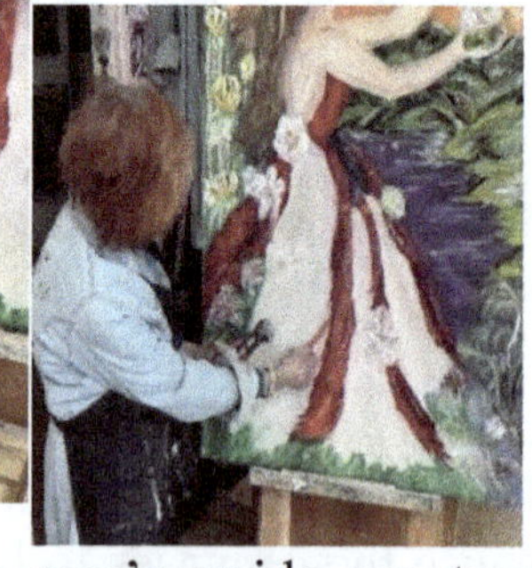

Directly behind the saw's guide are two examples of stone. The tall one on the right is a piece of marble about 8 inches tall. Next to it, is a large stone. Both must be sliced between one quarter of an inch to one eighth of an inch thick for creating pavements, roads, stone fences or brick buildings. The tile saw is very heavy, and all of my weight is needed to feed these hard materials through the blade.

Next, is an example of a large red glass shard, about 8 inches long. After carving on the bandsaw, the next step is to nip it into the final shape I need. After this, I decide where it will be placed. Holding the completed shard in my hand, I slowly move it over the entire painting. Should it go here, where I first thought, or somewhere else? Should it go on top of a shard already there to create depth?   How about here to add to a shadow? Maybe I need it in a slightly different shape?

Whenever a section of a GSP is not pleasing to me, I remove it. I melt the glue and scrape the glass away. Then, each shard is individually washed, possibly modified for the same piece, or stored for the future. At the end of a project the unused shards, including the tiny pieces, are saved in separate containers for another purpose, creating shadows, individual flowers, or ground to sprinkle on top of a painting or garden sections.

This discussion has been about the technical aspects of creating each GSP. It helps you to understand how I bring my art to life on the canvas.

Chapter Five: Selected Works, and Their Conceptual Development

This chapter is not about how to create a GSP. Rather, it is about enabling the bonds created between the GSP's and their owners. It is derived from letters, comments, and photos from them. Although I have given birth to each one, they now live with others. These examples of commissions illustrate the bonding between me, the GSP, and their new "parents."

The indelible bonding for the artist takes place with birthing the GSPs since all are the product of love and inspiration.

Every new owner has told me how owning a GSP affects them personally. Because of this, I decided to invite some of them to include their GSPs in this book and to share what these pieces represent in their lives. I sent them this letter:

"I am in the process of editing my book, *The Zen of Glass Shard Painting, and the Exploration of Creativity.* While doing this, it became clear that this book could not just be a 'how to'.

Before I regained consciousness from brain surgery, a voice told me that I was fine, yet the price to stay here was that I must learn to paint. I remember agreeing, with a brief flash of knowing this was probably just the beginning.

Developing the genre Glass Shard Painting was my response to that recollection. Unfailingly, I have been led and guided from my first attempts at painting through to this moment of writing, following what my mind and hands told me to do.

My life has journeyed, like others, along unfamiliar paths, participating in countless seemingly disconnected events. In time, I learned that everything contains opportunities for creativity. No matter how difficult it is or seems to be, the opportunity to learn is constant.

Relating major parts of my journey with the accompanying dynamics has led eventually to you owning your unique GSP.

My book is a personal story of my rebirth, an introduction to an unknown faction of myself and the process of the discovery and creation of GSP.

Each GSP contains a complete story. Since I cut thousands of glass shards, using my diamond-bladed wet saws and hand nippers, each piece includes my blood; this is unintentional.

You have honored me with having my creations in your home. I know that you care about the work as much as I do. Each piece is unique as are the owners.

I would like to ask you to send me a picture of your GSP with you standing next to it and say what it means to you, especially how the piece you own adds to your life.

With your permission, I will publish it in my book in a chapter talking about the pieces and your comments.

Thank you"

In the pages that follow the owners describe their thoughts and feelings regarding their GSP. These are personally meaningful experiences for them. For me their stories are both a privilege and a fascinating experience.

The first of my GSP commissions is chronicled below. I feel strongly that my spirit guides created this experience so I would learn to be comfortable creating works of art outside my box of familiarity.

<u>Deborah Illuminata</u>

Owner: Dr. Deborah Nightingale, PhD

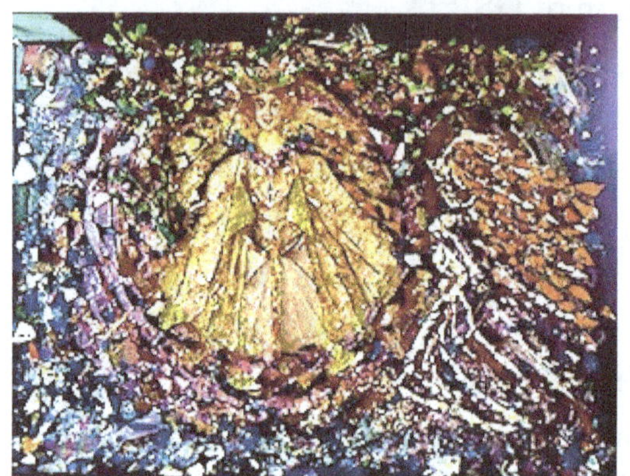

Deborah Nightingale wrote, "I had just spent 10 days in Glastonbury, England, the heart of the divine feminine goddess energy, and wanted to capture this energy in an art piece for my home. A message I received said I was to contact Eleanor to depict the goddess essence. It was pure joy to work with her creative genius to make the figures come alive in my "Deborah Illuminata" goddess glass shard piece on display in my living room! I feel its energy daily pulling me more and more into the goddess vortex!"

My thoughts: My first GSP commission, Deborah Illuminata was from my friend, Deborah Nightingale. My husband and I were attending a local musical event and invited Deb to join us for dinner before the concert. It was a lovely summer evening by the sea, as we sat chatting and enjoying a glass of wine before dinner.

She began to tell us about having just returned from Glastonbury in England, the home of the goddess of Avalon. I was deeply moved by this experience and the divine feminine energy permeating the entire site. Feeling a strong personal and spiritual connection, accompanied by the vision of her life there as a priestess, she asked me to create a GSP whose subject was the divine feminine goddess.

Listening to these experiences while visualizing them was almost hypnotic and I felt that I was there as well. Her request left me momentarily speechless. My first reaction was yes, followed by feeling on fire, excited, as if every bit of myself had sprung open to the thoughts, feelings, colors, and smells of Glastonbury. Knowing that my third eye had opened, I entered Avalon, and stepped into its magnificence.

I never doubted that I could do what Deb wanted, even though I had no idea of how. I just knew unequivocally She would emerge. Quieting down to the level of here and now, I asked Deb what she visualized and wanted. "An important element was fruitfulness.". In my mind, I saw the tree of life and its fruit. As she spoke, I began sketching on a napkin, asking the waitress to wait before we placed our order, saying, "I cannot do two things at once."

Before dinner ended, I said the painting needed to have her name as part of the title, and that I heard the name Debor-ah whispered in my ear. She exclaimed, "that's what my father called me.". Then I spoke of the piece being covered with gorgeous multicolored luminous glass shards. "Luminous" was another word we thought of in the title and I exclaimed, "Deborah Illuminata!" Deb said, "Great", and she was thus named before her birth.

I sent two different color studies of Deborah Illuminata to Deb asking her to choose the color scheme. She chose the study with an emphasis of red and yellow and together we picked out the primary colors of the glass which would create this unique GSP.

That night, I went to sleep asking my spirit guides to help me create the Deborah Illuminata. Eagerly, the next morning I set up my canvas and began to sketch what I had seen in my dreams. Using photos of Deb, I painted my vision of her soul merged with that of the goddess Deborah Illuminata. In the center of the picture was a fruit-full tree of life emerging from her crown chakra. My dreams showed her in her search for enlightenment with long red hair, streaming in the heavens towards her higher self. To emphasize her universality, longing, and movement towards her higher self, I "painted" her entirely with mirror shards. The mirror shards were also chosen so that each person looking into the mirror shards might see a reflection of their higher self.

The technique and method I used was to wrap large pieces of mirror in dish towels then smashing them with my mallet on my cinderblock.

This process was tremendously challenging since the pieces needed to fit together like a jigsaw puzzle.

At this time, I had never heard about diamond bladed water saws or hand nippers for glass.

Deb would come over about every 2 weeks and give me suggestions as to what to add and I would follow her directions faithfully. Finally, Deborah Illuminata spoke to me in a dream, saying, "I am complete".

The magnitude of Deb's generosity is a continuous inspiration. Both Deb and I know that our spirit guides helped me to move the process from start to completion.

When I think of Deb, I see her as an open conduit for the many enlightened spirits who communicate with her. Her extensive travels and unique spiritual experiences have introduced her to deep meditative states where she can hear and experience specific moments in time. Along with this, she is often given instructions regarding the integration of information, including healing, and raising energy to a much higher level.

As a result of these journeys, Deb commissioned me to do two more GSPs. These two figures have each affected the world profoundly. She has kindly allowed me to print them in this book.

Dr. Albert Einstein, PhD

Owner: Dr. Deborah Nightingale, PhD

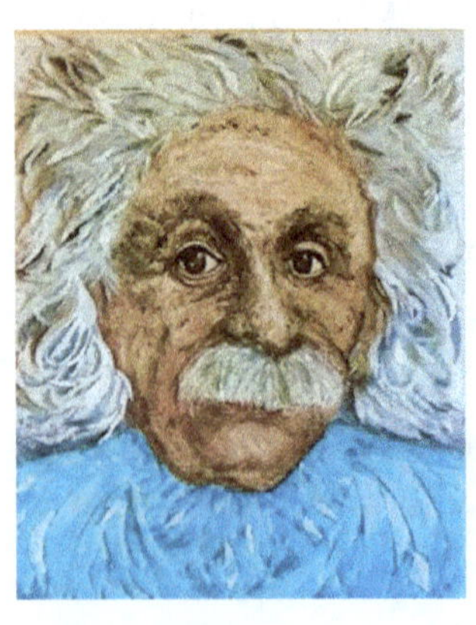

This GSP of Doctor Einstein was the second commissioned by my friend Deborah Nightingale. She had attended a workshop focusing on inspirations throughout life. While there, she talked about Dr. Einstein, his inspiration and that he was one of her spirit guides. Driving home, she stopped at an art gallery and saw a large, expensive poster of him and was greatly tempted to buy it. She did not. Arriving home, she was unable to forget the poster she had seen. The next day, she thought, "Eleanor can paint him; Eleanor can create Doctor Einstein for me."

My Thoughts: When Deborah asked if I could create a GSP of Doctor Einstein, I responded unhesitatingly, with an enthusiastic, "Yes!" However, I told her it would be a likeness as I interpreted him, not a portrait. Then went on to tell her my definition of a likeness: it expresses the eternal soul, is not static but alive and timelessly pulsating. Deb liked the sound of that and agreed. Shortly afterwards, we met, and she showed me several pictures of him. With his piercing eyes, wavy hair, and slight pixie smile, it seemed that he looked directly at me, saying, "Let's go!"

Obviously, Deb had a lot of confidence in me. She showed me various pictures of Dr. Einstein, while I found a few more. After placing about ten pictures of him on the table next to my easel, I felt unclear as to how to begin. Closing my eyes and meditating, I asked him for help. And, heard, "you will know and bring me to life. It will not be difficult. You will understand what to do."

Standing in front of my canvas, looking at the four photos I had decided to work from, his features appeared extremely distinctive, and immediately I felt relaxed.

It wasn't hard. While sketching his face and shoulders I decided that the background would be a light silver blue to complement his hair and eyes.

My first painting session after sketching and painting for three hours showed his face beginning to emerge.

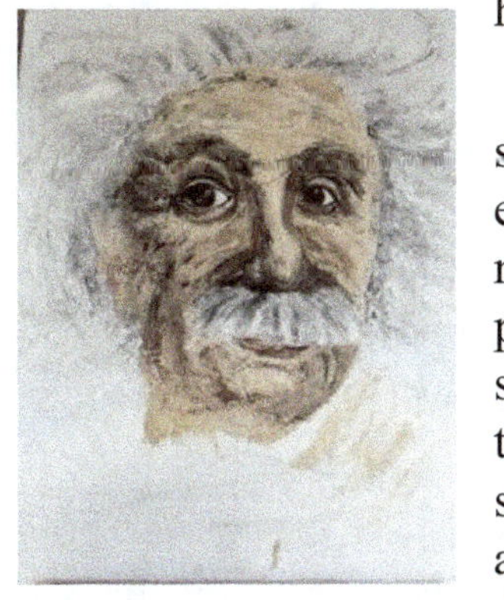

When doing a likeness, I make a quick sketch of the face shape and its features, especially the eyes. a basic skin tone comes next and then immediately afterwards I begin painting the eyes. The eyes of the subject speak to me and guide me. This picture on the left shows my first painting session after sketching. The eyes appeared slightly turned, as if he was communicating with another dimension, familiar to him, an aspect only he could see. Except for "glassifying" the eyes, they are exactly as I first painted them. I talk about my process and feelings to encourage people to work through their doubts and fears all the time saying, "You can do it" until it becomes intrinsic.

Doing "it", erases doubt. Corrections can be made any time with an attitude of openness to learning. Results will be much more satisfactory than if painted doubtfully. We know there will be a messy time, this is necessary. From chaos life will emerge.

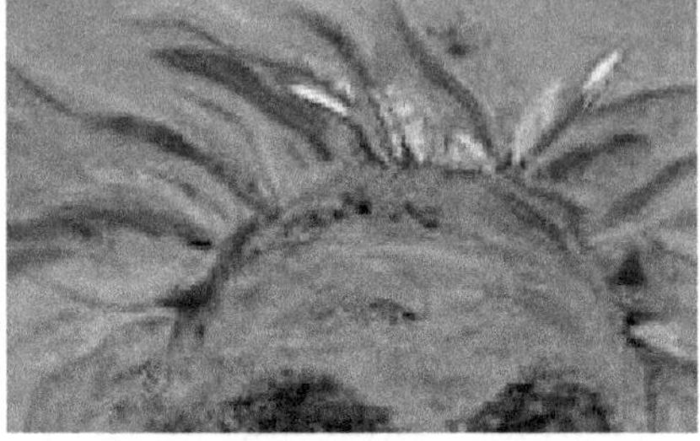

While I work, my concentration is intensely focused, causing the process to be physically exhausting, though at the same time I find it mentally and emotionally uplifting. After working for 2 to 3 hours, I take a little break. If time allows, I eat some food, close my eyes for 15 minutes and then resume for another two hours. Otherwise, I will continue working the next day. When I am involved in a project, I am excited and eager to continue. I do not procrastinate because like a seven-year-old girl, who is impatient to see what happens next, she is sure that when she finishes, she will have a delicious lollipop as her reward!

An important element of Einstein's classic visage is his unkempt but beautiful hair, which distinguishes him from his peers in physics, and just about everyone else. The "look" for Einstein I chose to use for my template showed that his hair was long, wavy, windblown, and layered with many colors containing white, silver, and gray of all different shades. The picture of his forehead shows the first layer of hair. Several pieces are iridescent, silver gray and white, placed throughout the entire head so the final effect is alive and multidimensional. You can almost see that it's a little windswept with the sun shining on him.

This image of his forehead also demonstrates how I began his hairline. Before it was complete, there would be about 200 more shards carved into the "hair" of glass, of every shape and tone replicating what is seen in the photo.

This next image shows me simultaneously working on Dr . Einstein's hair on his head and his mustache. The reason for this was to be clear that even though the glass texture is different from real hair, the colors are accurate, and pleasing to the senses. Each piece of glass is different and complementary on each side. Concentrating on both sides of the head, as the hair is developed, is invaluable in creating a harmonious and balanced picture.

The bottom of the photo shows his forehead with long carved pieces of glass shaped in wavy lines as I begin placing the curved shards. Deciding on the best placement can take a long time since the hair must look natural. The rest of his hair will be carefully designed in the same way to flow to his shoulders.

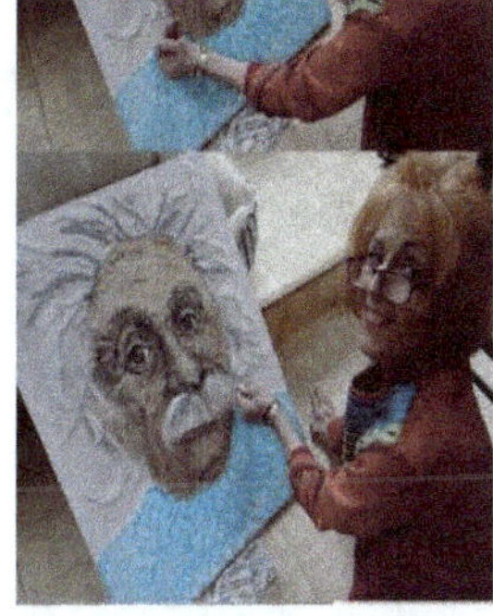

His mustache is composed of thinner, textured glass than that on his head, although with similar colors. The slightly different colors and thinner glass were called for since hair on various parts of the body differs in texture. Creating the hair and having it look real, presents its own unique challenge. sometimes four or five layers of glass were used to create shadow, depth, and a more realistic look.

I continue working until I hear, "I am complete". Dr. Einstein appears satisfied with himself.

<u>Mary Magdalene</u>

Owner: Dr. Deborah Nightingale, PhD

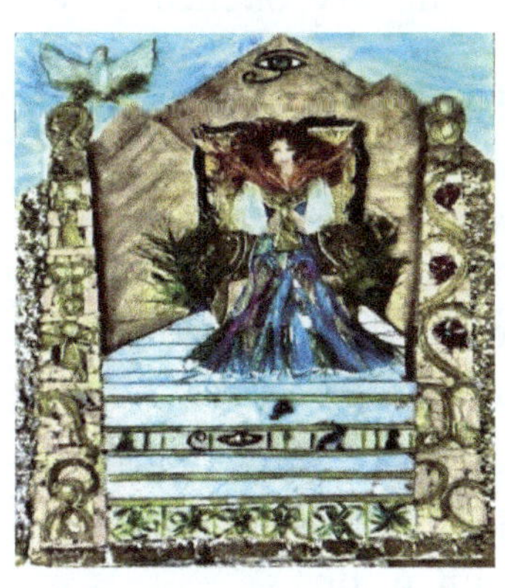

In Deborah's words: "Mary Magdalene is a complex piece of glass shard art that is full of symbolism and very personal to me. I have studied her for many years and made a pilgrimage to southern France to visit the sites where she lived following the death of her husband, Jesus Christ. She continued to preach his message of "love" until she died. Mary Magdalene trained in Egypt and, I too have a strong connection there, and thus the strong representation of the pyramids and the eye of Horus.

The white dove represents the "divine feminine", which she epitomized. Eleanor and I worked closely together to create the image

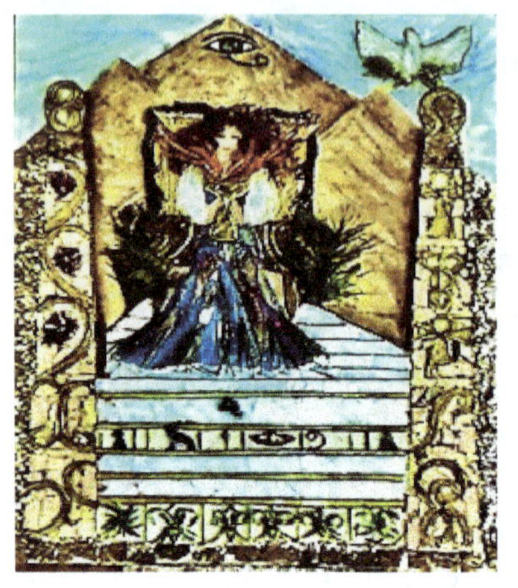

of both the divine feminine and the divine masculine as seen on the pillars on each side. The bottom contains multiple fleur-de-lis, representing the integration of the feminine and masculine. She is holding the "holy grail (chalice)", and the flames reflect the transformation of the world to higher dimensions. More symbolism of transcendence is contained in the peacock feathers and in the Egyptian characters spelling out my name, Meru.

Eleanor worked passionately to create this masterpiece which reflects not only the essence of Mary Magdalene, but also my personal journey. Her selection of the vibrant glass colors, coupled with the exquisite composition, have resulted in an amazing piece of art that I truly treasure!"

My Thoughts: My next commission from Deb was Mary Magdalene. When she asked me if I could do this my first thought

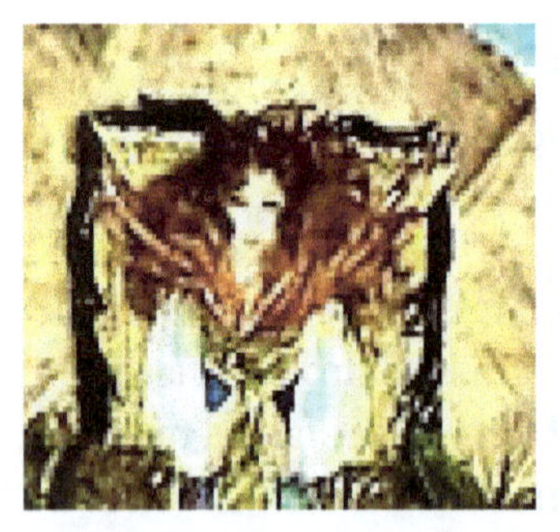

was, wow, what an exciting new experience! Of course, I said yes, knowing how much I enjoyed bringing people to life. Deb sent me references and along with my research, a door to another time and its history opened. My previous ideas about Mary Magdalene had been very limited. Who she was, the era she lived in, her personal influences, societal influences, customs, and traditions created an enormous puzzle whose pieces represented an entire culture? Deb requested several elements to be included, for example, a chalice filled with burning flames held by Mary Magdalene.

I chose to show her with long red hair as many pictures portray her. Her red hair is directly behind the extended flames, showing her as a vessel of world transformation to higher dimensions.

Knowing how connected Deb felt to this time and place, I asked if she would like me to merge her face with that of Mary Magdalene. An enthusiastic "yes", was her response. closing my eyes, I saw Deborah moving and being transposed on the image of Mary Magdalene, like a slow-moving film. It was as if I was watching her continuing her journey through many souls.

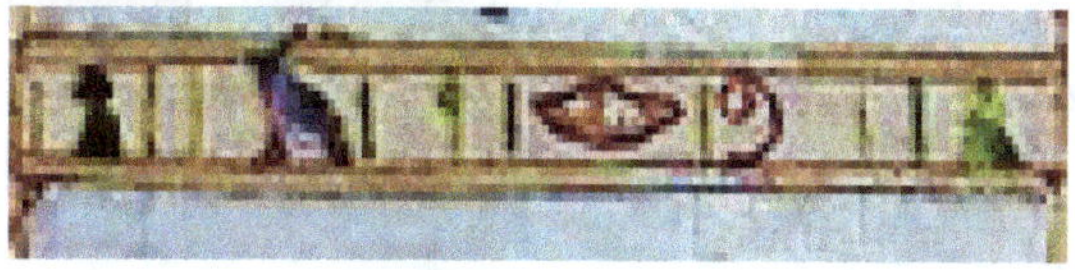

Another element Deb requested was the figure of a dove holding an olive branch, symbol of peace and the divine feminine. The dove is covered with several, layered, white iridescent glass feathers with slightly tinted blue glass.

Egypt is the site of this GSP, as many sources placed Mary Magdalene living in Galilee. The background is the Great Pyramid of Giza with the third eye at the top, symbolizing the higher self. The location of the upper Galilee is mountainous which is why I chose limestone in colors of beige brown and cream, a major anchoring element. The Great Pyramid is made up of thick pieces of these shades of limestone colored glass. Each piece was carved, guided by pictures of the pyramids. The pillars on both sides of the throne are made from the same limestone with inserts of pink, which is usually reserved for the sarcophagus. In between each stone and brick, I used pea stone of the same colors, sprinkling with my fingertips to achieve a look similar to the time and place. Each pillar represents the integration of the feminine and masculine.

The work was minute, arduous, and exciting as a first for me, creating the hieroglyphic name, Meru in Egyptian symbols in glass. Placed at the base of the throne, on the front of the stairs, Deborahs' name is there for all eternity.

50

<u>The Conversation</u>

Owners: Cheryl and Frank Conte

Cheryl wrote: "Frank and I loved the process of working with Eleanor on this work of art. She was so accommodating and gently offered suggestions that we include scenes and items which had personal significance to us. She also worked with us to ensure that the painting fit seamlessly with the specific decor, colors, and light in the room in which we were planning to display the painting. The scene is evocative of Italy, our favorite place, where we have visited numerous times. So now, every time we walk into our library, it reminds us of past and potentially future visits."

My Thoughts: The most romantic GSP I have ever created was commissioned by Cheryl and Frank Conte. I named it The Conversation. Their elegant, pristine home near the sea is filled with exquisite artifacts from worldwide travels. Each object has been chosen and placed carefully creating an ambiance of warmth and welcome.

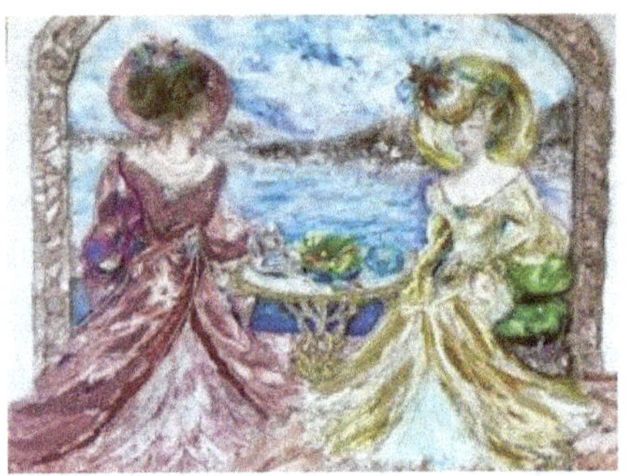

While visiting my studio, Frank noticed one of my earlier paintings of women and proceeded to tell me in detail what he liked and did not like as Cheryl attempted to prevent him from sounding critical. I loved his clarity and asked for more. Going to their home, I took many pictures of the room where the GSP would hang, the furniture and color scheme and photos of background elements.

We decided on a size that would look good on a fireplace mantle and I painted what I saw in my dreams. We had not discussed an exact motif except for some women outside and the ocean in the background. Learning that Frank had red/green colorblindness offered interesting challenges in choosing colors that would be acceptable, pleasing, and visible to him.

Painting the horizon line enabled me to see the roiling breakers across the bay on Nahant beach; strong unnamed feelings of familiarity emerged as the landscape outlines appeared. I could barely wait to see what the next stroke my paint laden palette knife would bring.

When the painting was finished, without describing it, I asked them to come over and tell me what they thought. Their reaction was positive, and they encouraged me to go ahead and begin creating the glass shard application.

I asked for as many details as they could think of since my goal was to create a GSP that whenever seen, said, "let's continue our conversation".

Before I begin creating the glass shard layers, I always ask if there is anything personal, they might like to include. In this case, the answer was an immediate, "Yes." What Cheryl wanted included in the piece was a lovely gold bracelet that Frank had given her before they were married. She said I could cut it up if I needed to, but I did not. I designed a dress with the bracelet as the neckline. There was also a pair of turquoise earrings, one lost, to use, then the other found, which was also included.

A request to use yellow in one dress and a red purple color from their carpet was helpful to anchor the designs of the clothes, furniture, and accessories, working well with its compliments. The color scheme felt like a jewelry box.

Between the figures of the two women, stands a glass and gold table like the one in the room where the new painting would hang. When I was taking the photos, I noticed that there was a vase containing some yellow flowers on top of the table. Noticing them, I decided I would enjoy the challenge of creating them especially since Cheryl loves yellow.

Cheryl's likeness came through easily, and I used her shade of blonde hair. Knowing her niece was coming to visit, I offered to paint her likeness expressing their warmth in an animated conversation.

The walls and floor of the veranda are tiny pink marble shards carved and interlaced with multicolor pigeon stone to create the right texture and sense of completion.

It is a beautiful day by the sea in the early 1890's. Two elegant ladies on the veranda, having conversation and enjoying a perfect moment in time.

The Conversation has many diverse elements, with six distinct areas. The anchor colors of red and yellow, two figures, a veranda framed with a marble arch, the ocean: a rococo style table between the two figures, and, the background showing a rocky formation, and the sky.

Cheryl's ensemble features a warm pallet of yellows with a touch of turquoise, as the complementary color. Her hat and gown were designed representing what two ladies of that era, and station in life would wear. With her light skin, and blonde hair, I visualized her in a yellow dress. Integrated in this unique objet d'art was some personal jewelry. Cheryl brought me the first piece of jewelry her husband bought her. It was a gold bracelet. Along with that was one turquoise

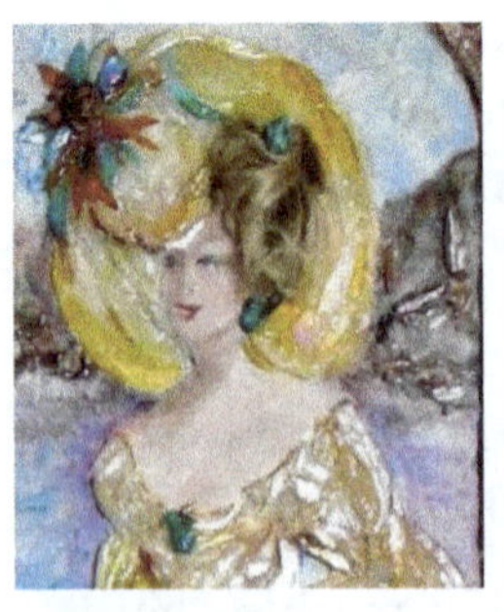

earring. As noted earlier I opened the bracelet into one long chain and used it as the trimming for her decolletage.

The fabric in both the hat and the gown are made from the same 'material.' Since the weather is warm, the bodice and sleeves of the gown are created from shards of iridescent glass to give the feeling of light silk. There are several shades of yellows in various tints and hues, with a touch of bright red orange balancing the bright red orange flower atop her hat.

A complementary color is the turquoise brooch at her neckline. The color turquoise is picked up on each side above her waist, calling attention to the fabric and detail. The elegant dress features lantern sleeves which billow out at the elbow, intertwined with pearls ending as a part of the wristband with a small bow over the button. A shard of turquoise glass is carved into a slight curve and placed at the top of the knee focusing attention subtly on the graceful folds of the dress. Cheryl sits on a small delicate settee whose fabric is shades of medium to lime green silk/satin, which helps to move the eye easily towards the green fruit on the table. While I was working on the painting Cheryl's niece was visiting, and I offered to create a likeness of her wearing the ruby colored dress. This suggestion was enthusiastically accepted. The dynamic color of the ruby shaded gown looks good against the background setting of the ocean. The bodice of her gown is silk lined with the same ruby color. It is high waisted, empire style with a belt featuring a diamond-like, square buckle. The sleeves are full and unique featuring harlequin shaped blocks of silk with colors ranging

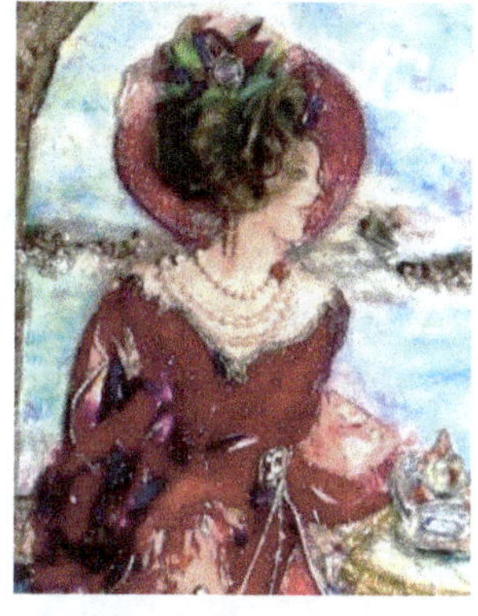

from deep ruby purple to a touch of bright pink. Since the sleeve on the right is glass and reflected in the sun, it appears to be a different color, but it is the same as the other sleeve. The texture of the glass used on the hat is straw – like, with a wide brim. Under the brim is a decorative arrangement featuring an amethyst brooch, and because of its position, the brooch is visible when the hat is worn directly on the top of the head. Her three strands of pearls are large, colored soft pink with a ruby brooch and drop earrings in ruby red. The trim on her neckline is diamante moving through the sleeves and down the front of her gown. The skirt of the gown is composed of two sections. The

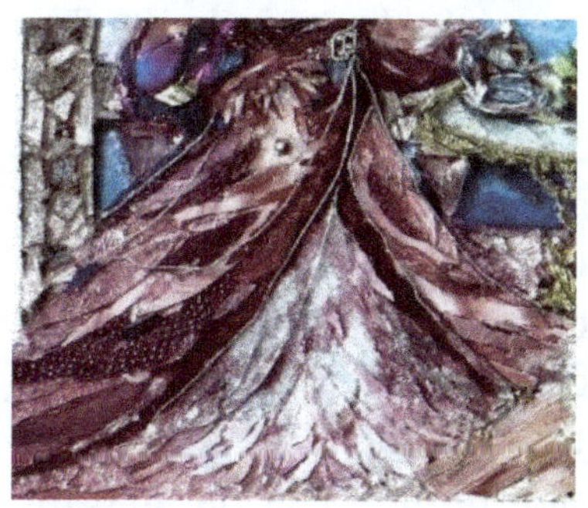

outer sections are created from colored glass panels of red, white, and pink silk taffeta, and the petticoat has the same colors only in much lighter shades. The lower section is outlined in diamante emphasizing the graceful curves of the draping fabric. The warm day we envision for this scene influences the design of this diaphanous gown.

The glass table with the food displayed between the two women

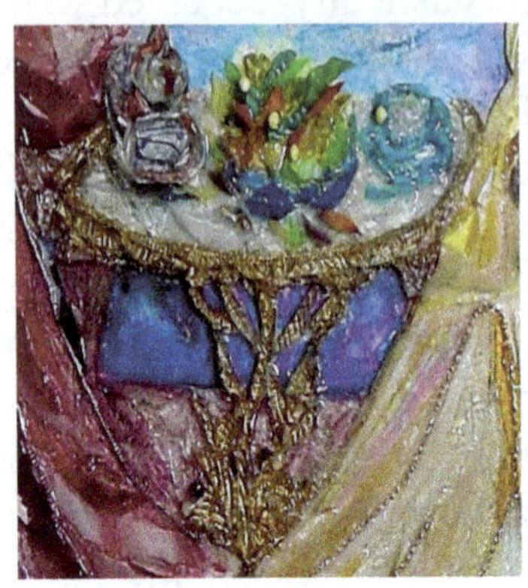

is a major focal point symbolizing that "the conversation" is pleasant where food and afternoon tea are enjoyed. While taking photographs of the room in which this GSP would be hung, I included a photo of this table. My interpretation of the table used the same appearance, textured, thick, gold colored glass. This glass needed to be cut extremely slowly on one of the diamond bladed saws and then the final shapes created with my hand glass nippers, using several small cuts on each shard so that the shapes would be clear, and pleasing to the eye. The tabletop is created from white iridescent large glass shards so that cups and saucers can sit comfortably. Atop the table is an attractive impressionistic arrangement, including all the colors in the entire picture. This element creates a feeling of a pleasant conversation.

This image is of a section of the arch on the veranda. To the right

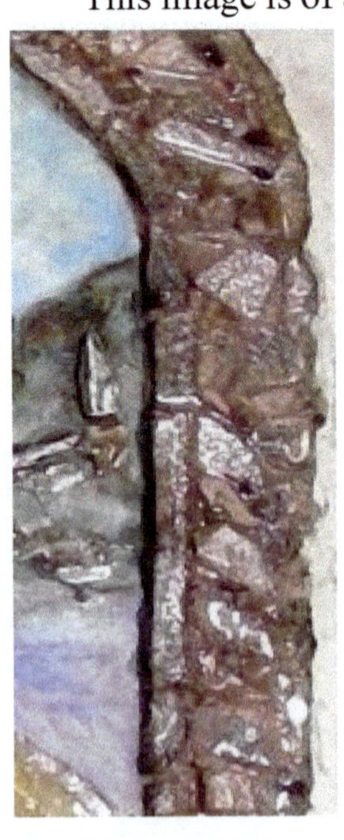

of the pillar is a small section of stucco, the material of which the entire home is built. The pillars in the arch have a small border on each side. This is made of pieces of pink marble (glass) which I sliced from a large block of travertine marble to 1/8" carved on the large tile saw. Inside these borders are shards of varying colors of pink marble with even spaces between them. I also used this treatment on the floor of the veranda, although the floor is flat and the marble stones within the arches are roughly placed. In between the marble shards are very pale "p" stones which I placed as in any authentic structure. The stones were also used on the veranda floor between the marbles and pressed down so they would be safe to stand and walk on.

The Countess Of Blytheswood

Owner: Gail Wilkinson

This GSP exemplifies the owner, an ageless, elegant woman. Entering her large and gracious reception room you are greeted by

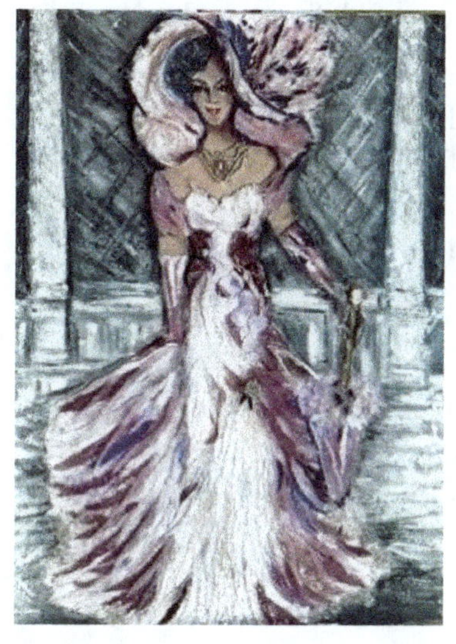

her 'likeness'. Her ensemble was designed using the colors associated with her family. Standing in front of her palazzo, she greets her escort as they leave for the fete on this beautiful warm spring day.

Creating this GSP, as in all others, begins first with deciding on the subject. Before falling asleep, I ask my spirit guides to help me, and this is what came through. "Follow your intuition, we are guiding you." With no idea in mind, I began sketching the next morning on a blank canvas using my T-square. What emerged were pillars and stairs. Seeing this, I decided this would be a palazzo and the background for Contessa, using her clothes to help tell her story.

The background is marbleized and textured iridescent glass which includes several shades of grays and white. The linear background is new for me as I am always drawn to the rounder shapes. Nevertheless, I enjoy challenging myself to do the unfamiliar. It is important to first decide upon a Statement Color in creating a GSP, as the glass is layered and multidimensional. Without one, it would be overwhelming and confusing. The word "balance" is always with me as I work. Deciding upon purple as the statement color holding everything together, gave me a great deal of leeway with shades, hues and textures using various shades of white as the complement and neutralizer.

The background is striking, strong and neutral, making this an excellent pallet for the colors and story. Next, I chose a color scheme to include hues and shades of purple, the colors associated with her family over eight centuries. 1890 Victoriana came to mind as the perfect timeframe.

Research began with familiarizing myself with the inner and outer garments and jewelry of that time so I could design a wardrobe appropriate to the season and her station. The Contessa wears an

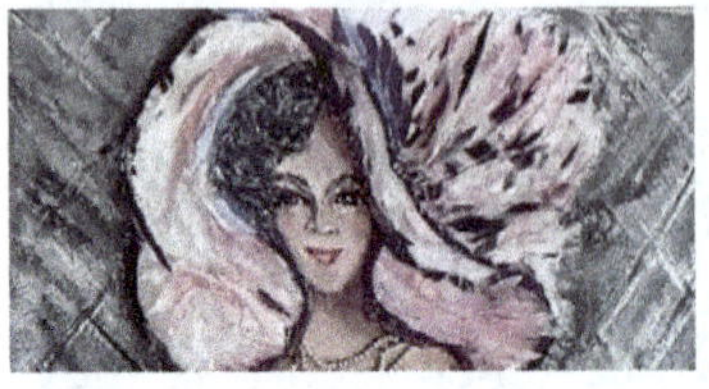

elaborate hat, with feathers, and an intricate diamond necklace. Her ensemble is created from at least eight sections of different glass shards and her gloves and parasol are unique. This process begins with first designing and painting the dress, hat and parasol and then visualizing the glass shards as the different fabrics needed for their design and execution.

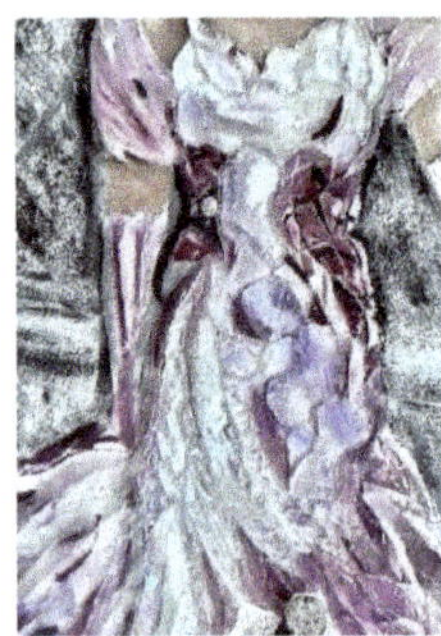

The top of the bodice is curved and carved from iridescent white glass which has inserts resembling lace. The lace looking bodice is carved with many minute snips as the garment is custom made, haute couture. On each side of the bodice are half sleeves, cut and shaped so that the glass looks draped with highlights and shadows, resembling heavy silk.

Directly under the bodice, the high waist was influenced by the previous Empire period. Below the waist the flowing and abundant material moves easily so that every step is graceful. Directly under the bodice, at each side of the waist, are shades of deep purple and iridescent dark blue. The small diamond brooch, at one side of the waist emphasizes her diamond and amethyst necklace, carrying the purple theme throughout.

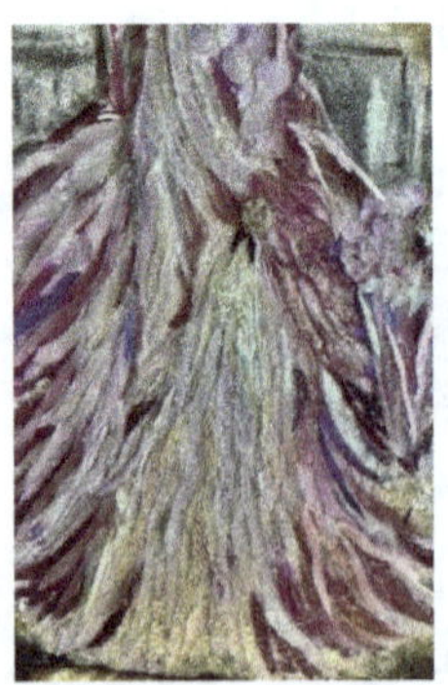

Between the side pieces at the waist an insert of iridescent white heavy silk begins moving towards the right side of her gown. Accompanying this is two more coordinating pieces gathered, moving towards the knees. Directly below the center insert is a large bow created out of heavy iridescent white and purple glass. This introduced the lower portion of the gown, showing that the gathered pleats from the left hip move towards the right side, caught by another diamond brooch over the knee, ending in a flourish of three ribbons.

Underneath the side gathers and the brooch, above the knee is another section created from sections of an irregularly patterned iridescent silver glass. This is interspersed with the same purple and white silk fabric as the rest of the gown. Just below the hips on both sides, the fabric billows out into a fishtail ending one inch above the toe of her slippers.

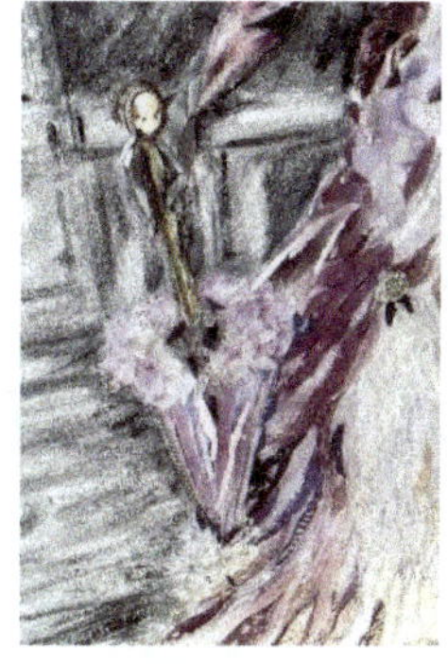

The parasol was designed to coordinate with the elegant gown of the Contessa. One of the few items which is not glass is the cameo on top of the handle. The parasol handle is made from a straight yet rounded long piece of gold brown iridescent glass. The ruffles are created from left over used pieces, creating the perfect texture. There is a strip of crystal stones on the side of the parasol showing that these strips are the bones interspersed throughout which keep the parasol secure and in place when opened.

The necklace was designed to follow the graceful lines of the gown. The center stone is a large, very deeply colored amethyst, carved as a chrysalis.

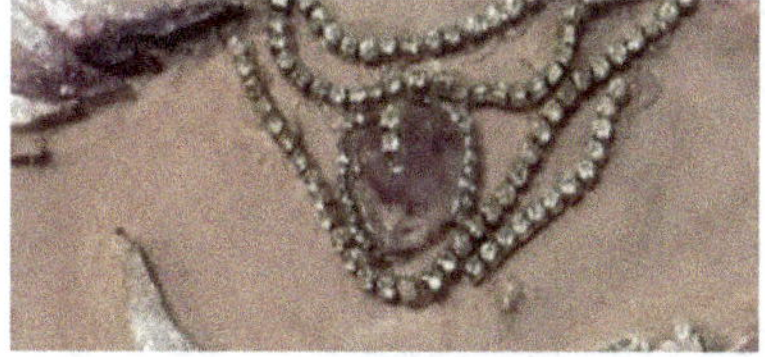

The gloves are of the same fabric as the gown. However, because the countess is known for her whimsical sense of humor, she decided that they be created differently. For sure they will be noticed, admired, and become the rage to be copied.

The size of the hat was carefully chosen to visually balance the entire ensemble. Beginning at the hip line, the gown begins to flare and taper in the back into a fishtail. The hat embraces all the colors used in the gown with the addition of bright deep blue. The touch of blue expresses her individuality, creating a complementary statement with soft lines. Each of the feathers are layered to add to the overall needed balance. The colors are swirled and carved to complement the lines of the gown.

The Story: The Contessa has lived a wonderful life. However, at this point her treasures are no more. Whatever can be sold is gone, only necessities remain. Because she and her family have been benefactors to countless others, people understand and remember. Finally, with one necklace and one elegant outfit remaining, she is attending, what she imagines will be her last society appearance.

Her plans are to sell this outfit and the last piece of jewelry the following day. Arriving at the garden party she is greeted with all the love she has extended to others.

Unbeknownst to her, a cousin of her former husband has arrived unexpectedly. Seeing her from a distance, the love he has always held for her causes him to approach, kiss her hand and say that his heart smiled. Time disappeared as they spoke.

Continuing, as they must, she invited him to return with her to her palazzo. On approaching, she said, "this is not as you remember it so many years ago." With tears in his eyes, he responded, "I remember I have always loved you," and asked her to marry him. She had been lonely as a widow for the last five years. As her eyes sparkled recognizing the mutuality of their love, she said, "yes.", and then whispered, "my beloved". Her palazzo began to fill again with remembered belongings.

Two months later, they were married at her palazzo. They spent their honeymoon on the Italian Riviera as the crew on his yacht tended to their every need, discreetly, of course.

Memories and Visions in Ice

Owner: Margaret Sisson

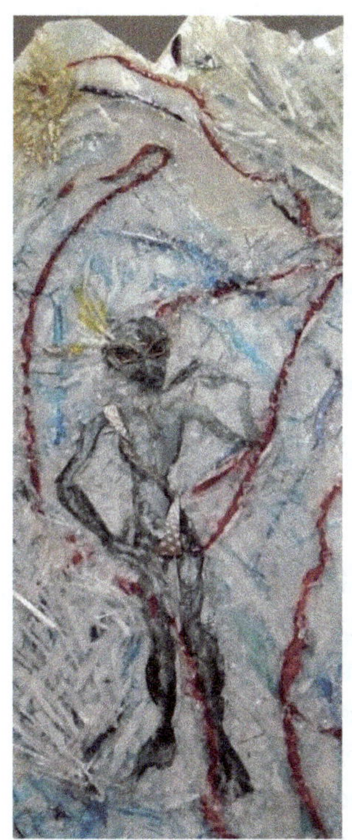

A unique woman asked me if I would create a GSP depicting Eskimos living in an environment which was predominantly ice. "Of course, I'd love to.", was my enthusiastic response. My Next question was, "Tell me about your idea and what you would like in the painting." She responded saying that her grandfather had been a physician to the Eskimos and ice was representative of the entire area. Additional elements to be included were a Martian, a specific cartoonish character, a hand pointing to Deer Island, an engagement ring, superman's fortress of solitude, a well-known musician, a red line, and the shining sun. It should also be large, capable of standing on its own, or hanging on a wall.

My Thoughts: Listening to Margaret telling this captivating story and the equally fascinating elements, my mind seemed to separate into two sections. Each element she described brought a picture with it.

Simultaneously, it seemed that I was visualizing and creating a custom-built canvas on which to tell the story. It needed to be large enough to carry the weight of at least three layers of glass shards of all shapes and sizes.

Drawing a picture of the canvas structure which I desired, I asked my husband Dennis if he could make this canvas from wood. He was able to build a jagged topped form, looking like an icicle. It was perfect; 2 ½ feet wide and 6 feet tall with a large stand on the back which could be folded flat to hang on a wall or extended so that could it stand on its own.

Now it was time to begin designing the picture. It took a long time, as there were so many segments to be included. The entire story needed to be clear with all the subjects placed in a balanced manner, 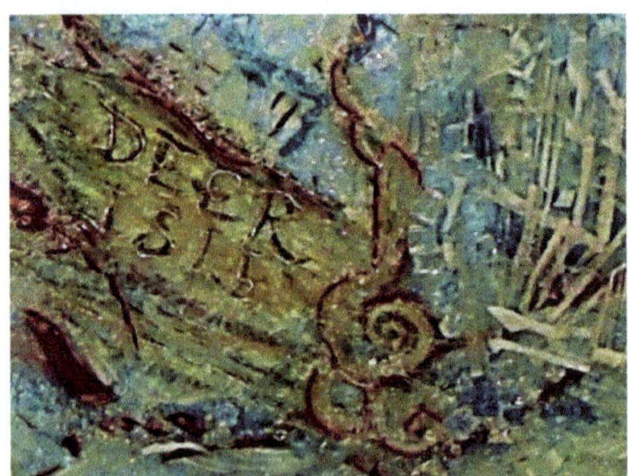 relating to one another as the visual story unfolded.

The following is a brief description of two of the elements: The sun was shining, consequently the Martian had sun's rays sticking out of the left side of his head; these rays served as an antenna, indicating his amazing intelligence and ability to gather information from every imaginable source. Naturally, with the sun's rays so strong he needed to have specially designed gold sunglasses.

The musician was indicated by a large treble clef and lines of music, a sign pointing to Deer Island where the musician lived.

After sketching and placing the various components, a link was needed tying everything together. I thought about the red line and its purpose. A meandering red line appeared in my mind, then I saw it meander throughout, touching our subjects, then moving on. This red line would represent life, precious memories 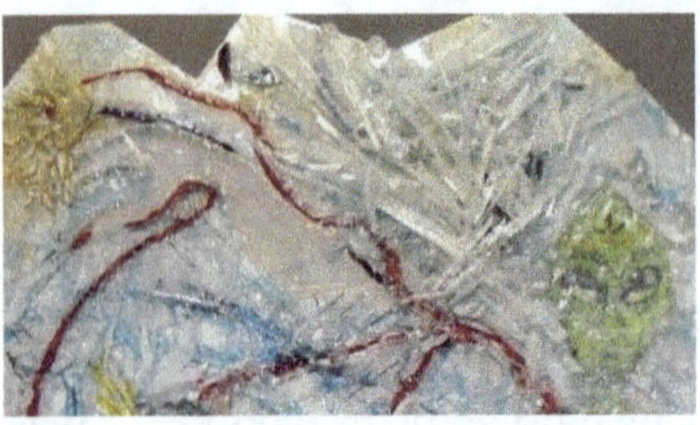 and heartbeats which go on forever. The flowing red line also signified and assured eternal connection.

Margaret's Vision - The Iceberg

Owner: Margaret Sisson

Special challenges, and unique projects have always excited me. I love to go to the place of, "never done it before.". It is exhilarating, another opportunity to learn, an exploration and my interpretation of, beautiful.

Margaret again asked me, some months later, "Can you make me an iceberg?" "Wow!" I thought. And replied, "Sure, what exactly do you want and how big? Let's do it!". This is my usual response, knowing the exhilaration I feel when I have come to a new door.

The family history continues with Margaret's request that I create an iceberg and she proceeded to tell the story that informed me why it was meaningful to her. The story has been passed down to the present day in Little's family letters.

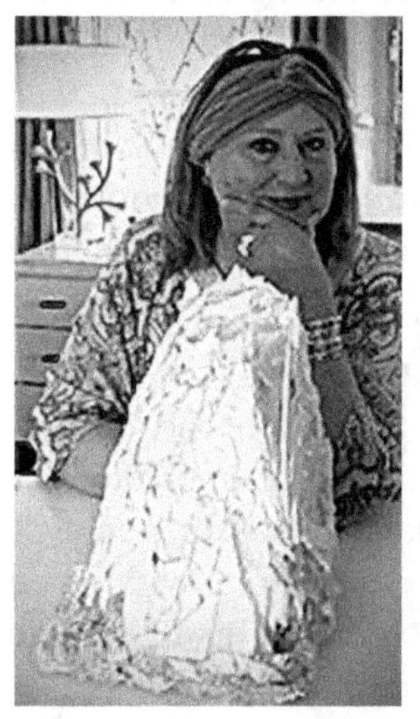

In 1912 the Titanic was four days out of Southampton, England bound for New York when it ran into trouble. At the same time, off the coast of Newfoundland, Margaret's great grandfather John Mason Little of Boston and Swampscott was at the helm of a steamer, sailing from New York headed east to England. He was present when the distress call came in from the Titanic. Looking at John, the captain asked, "what should we do, my guests paid a lot of money for this trip." John's immediate reply was, "you have no other choice but to do the right thing". The Titanic sunk in the early hours of April 15, 1912, after sideswiping an iceberg during its maiden voyage. The chaos resulting from this disaster was unthinkable at the time. The supposedly unsinkable ship was going down! Of the 2,240 passengers and crew on board, more than 1,500 were lost. Margaret's ancestor was among the first to arrive on the scene to help the survivors and she felt the image of an iceberg would be a fitting memorial to the passengers, crew and rescuers who were apart of this tragedy.

There was one requirement in creating the iceberg, and the rest was at my discretion. Margaret sent me a corbel to use as a form with the instructions that the dimensions were to be no more than sixteen inches high and 12 inches deep and completely white.

My Thoughts: Before beginning I had one thought. It would be my frame of reference and guide me. This was, "the memory of this iceberg is ageless, and an integral piece of forever." With that knowledge in mind, feelings of satisfaction and excitement flowing through me, I began. I looked forward to the challenges, which I knew were there however yet unknown. The following photos show the process and steps used in its creation.

The inner form of the iceberg is a wooden corbel with a flat back and a rounded front extending 7inches deep and 11 inches high. This

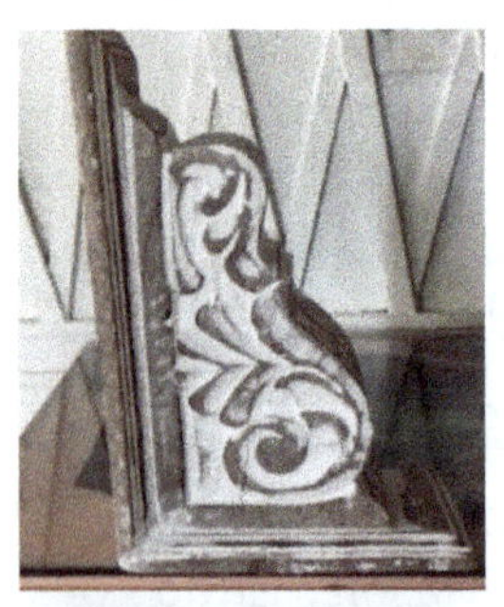

image shows the corbel form sitting on a wooden base. It will remain and be part of the finished iceberg. The first step in building the iceberg was to cover the corbel entirely with three thick layers of tinfoil, placed in various configurations to provide places to begin attaching the glass shards.

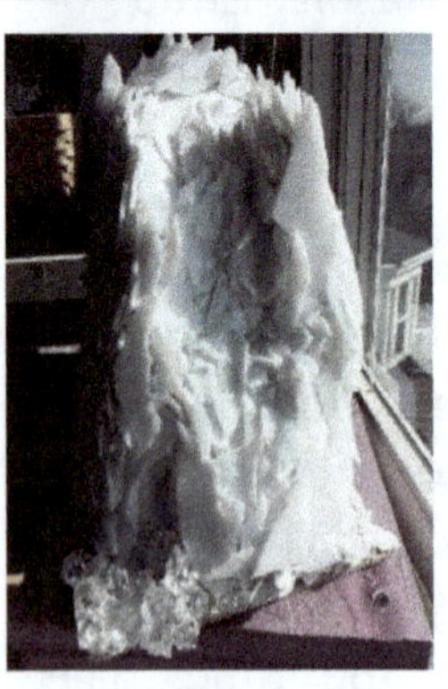

This photo shows the sturdy base I covered with larger glass shards with several shards at the bottom to begin laying out the base of the iceberg. The slightly hollowed section is an indicator for windswept chunks which have been removed over time. The structure is then covered with large shards of glass which serve as margins that guide me. The purpose for the large base shards is that they create a firm foundation on which smaller shards will be affixed. The design will continue to take shape in that manner, adding smaller ice shards on top of each layer.

I ground glass into pieces resembling coarse salt and then sprinkled them with my fingertips over parts of the iceberg. More than five hundred glass shards were cut and shaped with my glass nippers to create each individual shape. The larger saw was used to carve most of the shards. However, the bandsaw was used for more delicate small pieces. I created crevices which have been shaped by the elements. At the top a few icicle shapes have been placed as a guide where more will be added. The iceberg is not yet balanced and appears top-heavy. Visual balance and weight will be achieved by carefully layering individual glass shards around the structure.

Not just white, but colors of many shades and textures, along with their careful placement allows the dimensions and shadows to be imagined as the sun shifts direction over the iceberg.

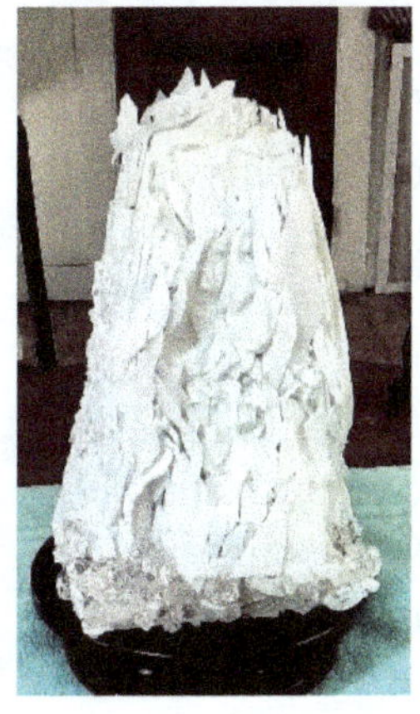

At the bottom of the iceberg a large deep V-shaped has been hollowed out and is often used as a shelter. On completion, a long icicle on each side will frame its entrance. Directly below that is the example of two ice blocks, which I will use around the base to finish it. The placement will tell me how many to use and the shape of the design. Creating the iceberg called for at least four to six layers of various shades and textures of white glass shards combining them into a completed piece of forever.

Sprocka

Owner: John Sprocka

Commissioned by Peggy Schrage

One of my favorite art endeavors is creating a GSP for someone. I feel honored to be chosen and entrusted to create a work of art which 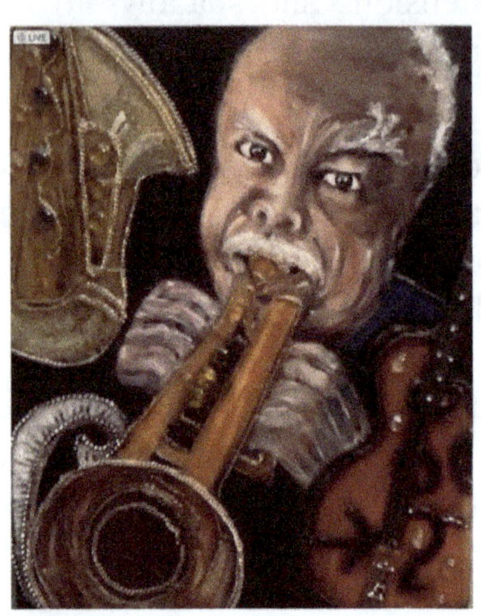 means a great deal to a person. A friend of mine, who is also a client, Peggy Schrage, told me about a very talented musician friend living in Antigua and wanted to give him a gift in gratitude for the pleasure his music had provided over the years. She continued, saying that "he plays several instruments including the piano, guitar, flugelhorn, and trumpet. He also sings." "That's fascinating," I said. "What's his name?" "Sprocka," she replied. I paused for a second and looked out of my studio window over the ocean's horizon, realizing that I wanted to connect with him. Peggy said, "I'd like you to do a GSP of him including all of his instruments." "I'd love to.". I replied, then said "I need to have several pictures of him, including one playing a horn and facing forward. I said," Peggy called him, told him what she wanted, and, in a few weeks, she brought me the pictures. Laying the pictures on the table, I decided that his likeness playing his flugelhorn would be the centerpiece with the other instruments surrounding him.

My Thoughts: It took about a week to create a balanced composition which included every instrument. It was also important to create an interesting scene which would tell a story. This took about a dozen large sketches before work began on the canvas.

The color of one photo was black and white; several others were unclear. Calling Peggy, I asked, "what color is Sprocka?" Peggy said, "I never even thought of it."

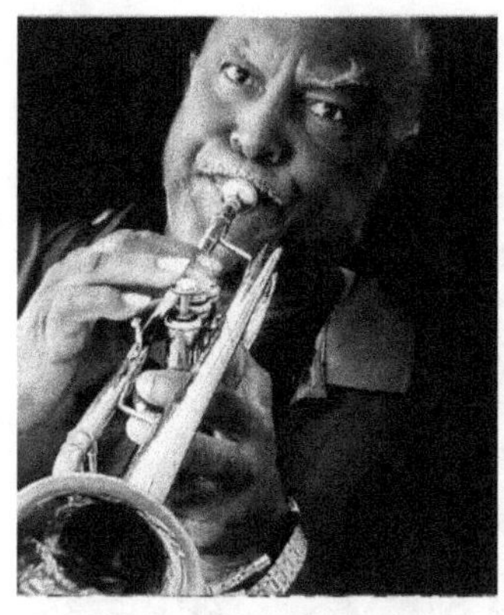 After much discussion we settled on the lighter reds of the majestic Arizona mountains. I felt mystified knowing that the right shades and hues were needed so that Sprocka could be heard playing his instruments. With shades of umbers, reds, yellows, blue and white on my pallet, experimenting with various amounts, eventually a basic skin tone emerged. On this highlights and shadows would define the unique planes and curves of his face. After I finished the painting Peggy came over to approve it before the next step. She loved the painting, enthusiastically, saying the painting caught him exactly.

The next phase began by selecting the colors for the instruments. Because there were different instruments of varying sizes, selecting their colors was complicated. Their shapes and their shadows needed to be accurate to suggest their individual purpose. Because each instrument is composed of sections, several patterns for each instrument needed to be accurately drawn and created. Then the glass cut into shards on the band saw, hand trimmed with the nippers and finally each piece fitted together like a jig saw puzzle. This was a required, precise, time-consuming process of more than 10 hours for each instrument.

Finally, the day came when Sprocka visited Peg and she told him she was bringing him over to see a picture of a "bird" I had painted. When he arrived at my home, he was invited up to my studio where I had a towel covered presentation waiting for him. He sat down and my husband filmed the whole event. Included are several photos showing the presentation to Sprocka.

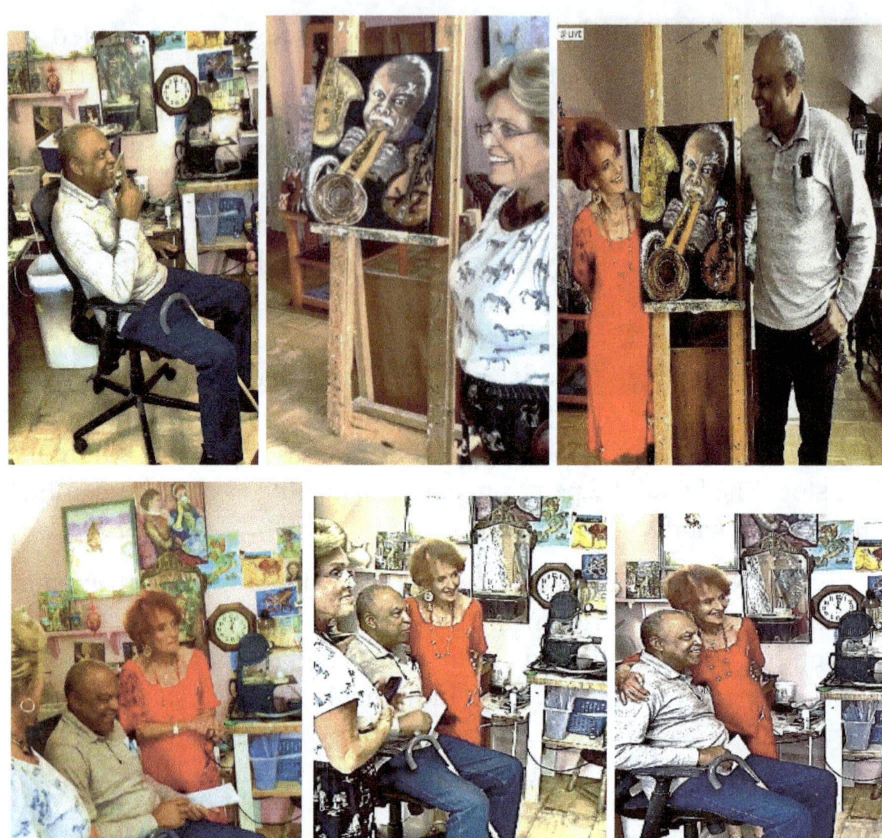

Overcome with emotion after seeing his likeness with his instruments, he asked, "How did you do this and why?" He could barely contain himself. I said, "wait a moment I wrote you a letter answering all of your questions."

"Dear Sprocka, Peggy asked me how I would feel about creating a glass shard painting of a musician friend of many years who lived in Antigua. I said, "of course, I would love to. Quickly adding the caveat, it will be a likeness not a portrait. A portrait captures an impression at that moment. I feel someone's energy, dream about them, and communicate with them out of body spiritually even though we have never met. Peggy has always referred to you as Sprocka and I have come to know you that way. Because of its lyrical sound, your name has provided me with other information about you. I loved creating

67

your likeness and getting to know who you are. I think the biggest challenge I had was asking Peggy what color you were and finally settling on the colors of the high majestic mountains in Arizona. Please enjoy your glass shard painting. It is unique, as are you. It cannot be replicated in any way, and this is also true of you."

Namaste and love from Eleanor Fisher

Coco

Owners: Katerina and Anna Nemshati

Kat's Boutique, Swampscott, Massachusetts

Katerina wrote: "Coco brings endless joy and personality to Kat's Boutique. Your glass shard portrait of Coco wearing my beautiful pearls has made my lifelong dreams of her come true.

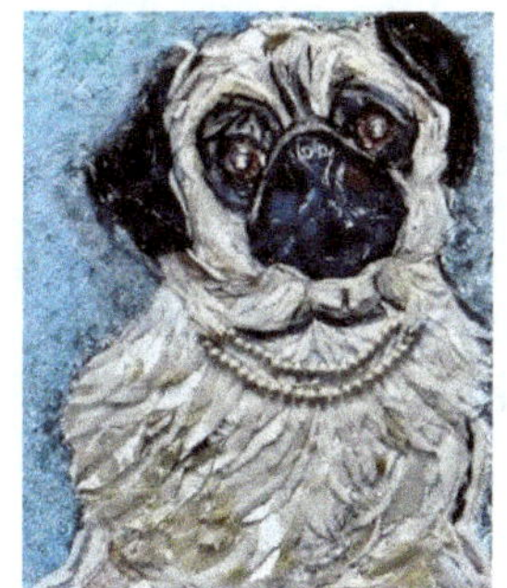

Coco's sparkling glow shows her unique personality. She is truly one of a kind. At Kats, Coco's portrait will always be cherished. Thank you, Eleanor, for your passion and fabulous work.

Katerina and Anna"

My Thoughts: Kat had seen my GSP of animals and showed me a picture of a gorgeous white French Pug that she wanted me to paint and 'glassify'. I was happy to accept the commission as creating portraits of animals allows me to show their unique personalities. "Is there anything you would like me to include in the picture?" I asked Kat. She replied, "just my pearls for her to wear." "You mean put them in the picture?" I asked? "Yes", she unhesitatingly said. I said, "What if I need to cut them"? "That's fine," was the response.

My first task was to research the personality of the French Pug. It showed that the French Pug is playful and fun with physically distinctive features, has a fine, glossy coat that is most often fawn or black, and a body with well-developed muscles.

Sounded perfect to me, since the dog and owners are often quite similar. The description of the French Pug was a description of Kat and her elegant, fun, boutique in Swampscott, Massachusetts.

Kat is physically distinctive with her lean shapely dancers' body and long blonde hair, often in a French twist, wearing pearls. She is a talented pianist and teacher, always smiling along with her equally stunning daughter Anna who greets you as you enter the atmosphere of this fun and elegant boutique.

Looking into the eyes of Coco, you know she is alive and happy. Coco is the essence of Kats Boutique, and everyone who enters receives at least two welcoming smiles.

Goddess Alessandra

Owners: Sandra and Jonathan Willmer

Sandra wrote: "I am the proud owner of this incredible painting, 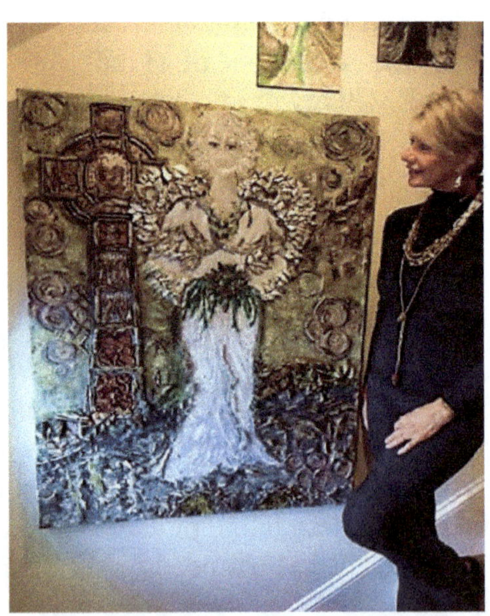 Goddess Alessandra! I was Eleanor's model for the piece and am honored to be Alessandra's embodiment.

She hangs in my entrance hall, is the first thing I see on coming in, and she represents my porthole of strength, security, and encouragement. I love the story of her history, and experience, and feel her energy always. This piece has inspired me so much with my own painting as well as my jewelry design, for which I'm profoundly grateful.

She brings me so much joy and I absolutely love having her with me and the grounding she represents. Thank you, Eleanor! "

My Thoughts: Outside the entrance to the Irish National Heritage Museum in Wexford, Ireland stood an angel about six feet high. It stopped me in my tracks. While it was of plain gray granite, composed only of several basic, sensuous shapes and curves, her elegance, strength, and timelessness spoke to me. It was as if we knew one another at a different time. She had been immortalized. There was no doubt that on returning home, I would attempt to capture her essence on a large canvas. I was awestruck, flooded by an overwhelming sense of the 9,000-year history recreating Ireland's heritage in this outdoor museum. As my husband Dennis and I walked here, and later at the hills of Tara site, my finger seemed frozen to my camera as I attempted to capture what I was seeing and feeling. Tara transports us back 6,000 years when the first settlers came. At the entrance stand two stones. The taller of these two is thought to feature a figure of the Celtic fertility god Cernuous.

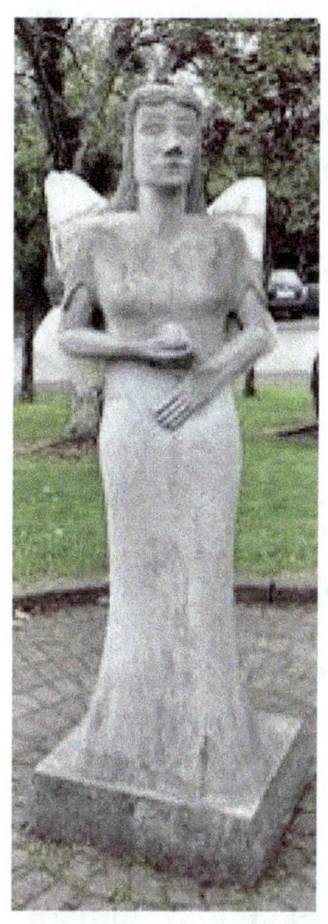

The hills of Tara, sacred and royal was the place that 142 kings are said to have reigned in the name of Tara and revered as a dwelling of the gods. Here, the most powerful Irish kings held their great inaugural feasts and were approved by earth mother goddess Maeve.

Visiting the Irish National Heritage Museum and the hills of Tara left me with indelible impressions and memories. Having so many deeply felt personal and spiritual experiences, I began to dream about how to describe the essence of this amazing trip through the ages.

What could I do to bring the spiritual, intellectual, and emotional sensory experience to life was the question I asked myself repeatedly?

Some of what I saw included the Celtic cross with pictures representative of daily existence carved in each quadrant; the Celtic hieroglyphs; the call of the goddesses, gods, and spiritual energy. There was a sense of urgency and personal challenge in bringing these objects to life. I knew that I wanted to find a way to acknowledge these people and their journey.

Before falling asleep, I thank my guides for their help and ask for continued direction. Sometimes I do not hear answers, yet the work continues even though I don't remember hearing anything. Answers come in many forms. My dreams are always in color. Often, I will hear, "you're doing fine, don't worry, we'll continue to guide you". Soon after returning from Ireland, a brief message came from my spirit guides, "Use a model." I heard myself exclaiming in my sleep, for what? I've never had a model, just me. The response, "You said you wanted to represent what you saw in Ireland." How am I supposed to represent what I do not know? "You will think of it tomorrow." The answer came before my dream thought finished. "Do it, you'll learn, we'll guide you". The usual.

I kept looking for a model unsuccessfully. Then a few months later at Marblehead Arts Association, I saw a stunning tall blonde woman, and I heard, "That's her". "But I don't know her," I responded. "You will, she's your sister". "Right!", I thought. The entire conversation took place in a fraction of a second.

After meeting casually at some art shows we became acquainted. I told her the story of the angel and showed her my photos, explaining I never had a model before, followed by asking her to model for me. By that time, I knew I wanted to create a statue like figure which would be my Tara. My goal was to create her as pulsing and calm representing the timelessness, strength, essential elegance, and the nurturing instinct of women. The name of my model is Sandra and she said she would love to be the model of the goddess Tara. That was the beginning of a wonderful friendship.

A new chapter in my life began, filled with growing inspiration and creativity. Many firsts occurred at that time; my first model and first experience of carving stone and recreating the small pictures embedded in the Celtic cross.

Sandra was the perfect person to have for my model; highly spiritual, helpful, patient, intelligent and our energy was completely complimentary. She was fascinated by the process and what we were creating together. The goddess Tara took shape and began to emerge on the first day. On our second sitting, Sandra said she wanted to buy the piece. Three people were in my studio; Sandra, me, and the goddess Tara and all agreed that was a wonderful idea. She helped me pick out the perfect iridescent blue shards for the goddesses' eyes. (We both have blue eyes.) Every day I sent Sandra photos of the goddess. Sandra's persona is a part of a continuum of forever. Early one morning towards the goddess Tara's final completion, the sun had risen in my studio shining directly on Tara.

The morning after her completion, I entered my studio and saw the sun sparkling on her, the emerald necklace and the bouquet of trailing vines encompassing the shamrocks of Ireland. I was personally there with a timeless presence.

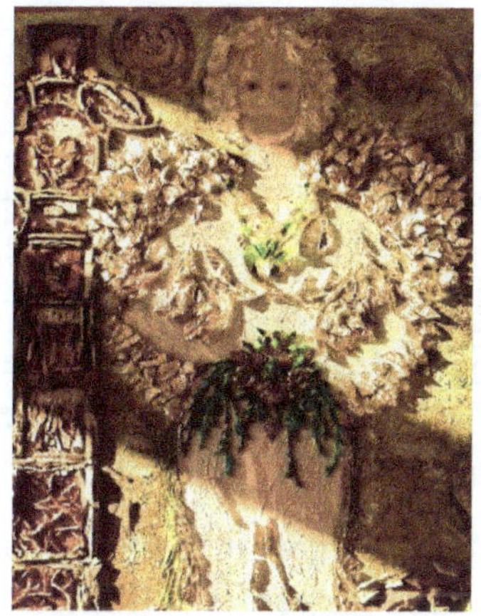 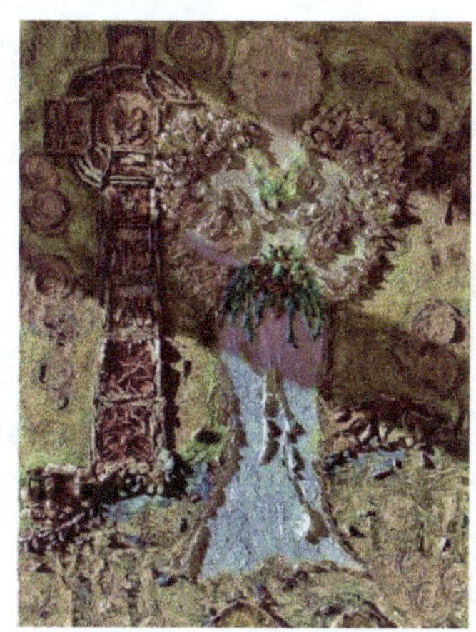

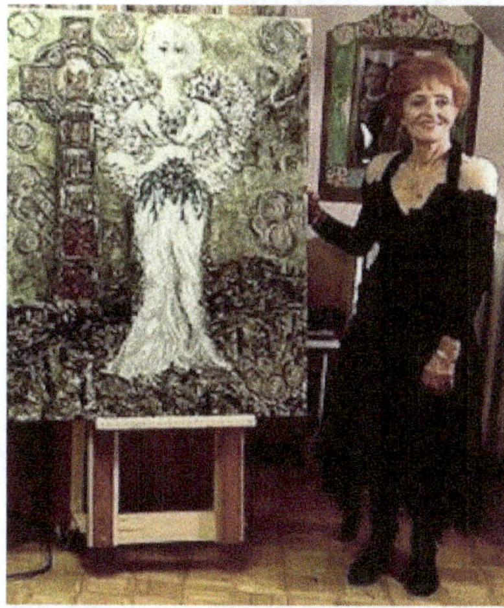 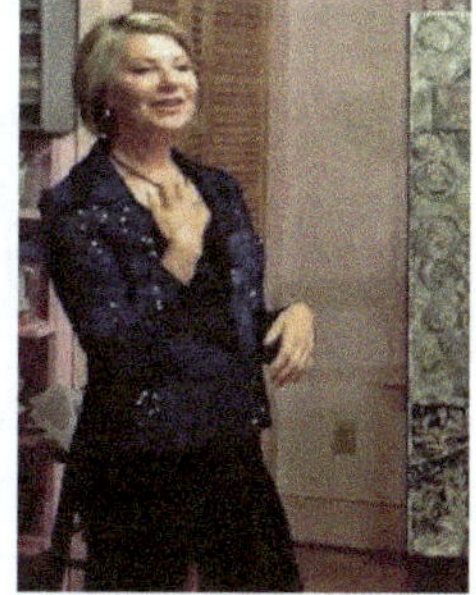

The goddess Tara was presented to Sandra at an intimate gathering befitting her birth. Her new mother named her Alessandra, and all raised their glasses.

<u>Wisdom</u>

Owners: Lynda and Jim Kerscher

Unexpected connections can bring wonderful gifts. What follows is a story of unexpected connection leading to new friends.

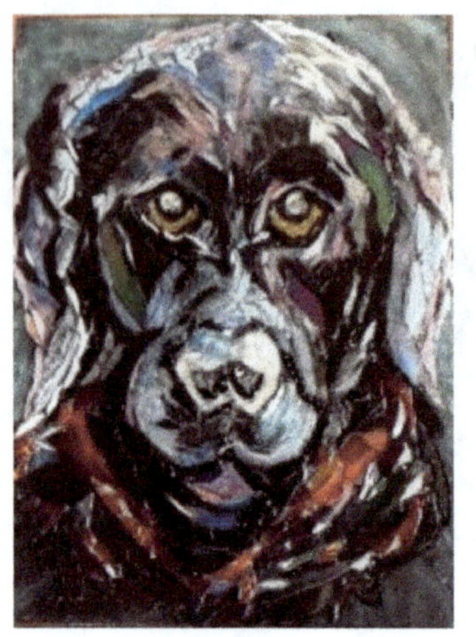

I have always loved animals and could not let go of the idea of painting a Labrador, my first painting of such an animal. When finished, I posted my GSP of this Labrador who I named Wisdom on my website. A woman who visited my website saw Wisdom and inquired about him. We spoke several times as I told her about the development of GSP and the unique Labrador who was so attractive to her. She and her husband decided they would like to own Wisdom.

It was their first experience buying something expensive from a stranger a thousand miles away. As soon as Wisdom arrived at their home, they opened the package and could not believe their eyes. Lynda and Jim's reaction was that he was alive, and they loved him.

Now begins Lynda's voice telling the story of connections. She wrote, "The story of friendships, love of dogs and special people with artistic talents bringing joy across the miles. When we moved to Rome, Georgia we became friends and neighbors of Glendene and her husband Bill. Later, Glendene met Nancy and Max , who became second parents to Glendene and Bill. Becoming acquainted with Eleanor's unique talent, we purchased a glass shard Painting, entitled "Wisdom," whose subject was a black lab. When he arrived at our home, we immediately loved Wisdom, feeling his humanity and lovingness. We told our story and shared our beautiful work of art with Nancy who was deeply moved by the feelings Wisdom evoked in her.

A few months later, Glendene's special dog, a Chihuahua named Sugar passed to doggy heaven at the age of fourteen. After seeing Wisdom, Nancy knew that she wanted to have Eleanor create a GSP of Sugar. This was to be a special Christmas gift for the couple she had grown to love and consider an integral part of her family. The connection between Sugar's and Wisdom's portraits, has reaffirmed an enduring re-connection of three families. Our families have been close for 40 years. The portraits of Wisdom and Sugar celebrate the uniqueness of our relationships. And, now we add a most special artist and her husband to our treasured friendship from over one thousand miles away.

W- is for the wonderful acquaintances we have made after fifty-two years of marriage who have come into our lives through the mystery and creativity of the art world. These are two people who have reignited our belief in trust, honesty, kindness, and generosity shared.

I- is for the idea of playing Words With Friends with a very special lady named Faerie Flower.

S- is for serenity and peace Wisdom, the Lab has provided us since March,2018

D-is for dog which spelled backwards is god, representing patience, and love without judgement, constant companionship and one who listens to your every prayer.

O-is for how often we go astray in our journey of life but by the wisdom of others, if we listen, will bring us back on track.

M-is for the many blessings we have been given including our two sons and grandchildren, wonderful and lasting friendships along with many rescue dogs we have and adopted for which wisdom the dog reminds us of every day."

My Thoughts: While growing up, many of my friends owned pets. My neighbors raised Labradors. I remember being four years old and going to visit the six new puppies. Five of the litter were sold and I called the one which remained, my boy. I held him when he was first born and visited him almost every day.

On my birthday, I awoke to find him sitting next to my bed in a basket with a purple polka dot bow on his collar. The next year when I was five, I decided to celebrate our birthdays together and gave him a biscuit. However, first I bit into it to show how much I loved him and said, "this is delicious. Now, it's yours, happy birthday, my boy". I am sure that memories of him guided me to paint the soul of the Labrador which shines through his eyes.

(As this book goes on sale, my friend Lynda has passed to spirit. I feel her with me and know she and Wisdom are together).

<u>Sugar</u>

Owners: Glendene and Bill Naguszewski

Bill wrote: Dear Eleanor, your Glass Shard portrait of our Sugar

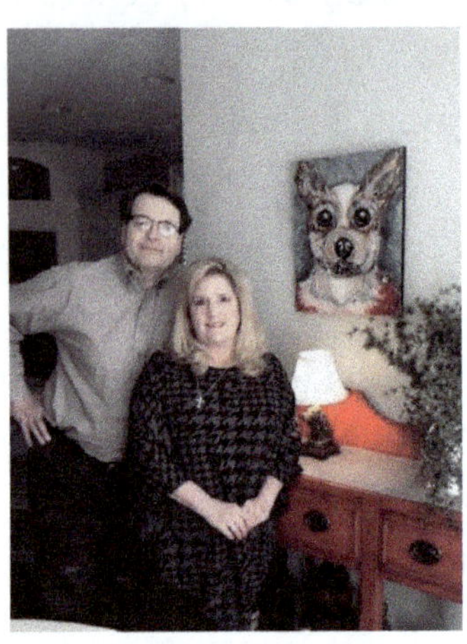

warms our hearts each morning and as we return home at night, displayed prominently on the wall that is the fulcrum point of the kitchen and the family room where we spend most of our time at home. We lost Sugar in august of 2018 and it is so difficult for Glendene to talk about her still without crying and tears flowed from our eyes when we received her portrait, we were not blessed with children but have been fulfilled with a marriage of 25 years and by the love of our pets that we have a passion for rescuing.

Glendene's grandmother had always wanted a lap dog and we found Sugar for her. Grandma loved Glendene very much, however we lost grandma six months later. Sugar thus became ours. The two were inseparable, each being identified as part of the other. Glendene and Sugar were always giving each other "rapid fire kisses," singing together or dancing. Sugar never felt it proper to be undressed or underdressed for the occasion whether to go to bed with Glendene or to our neurology practice. She was our Lady Liberty on the Fourth Of July, the good witch of the east at Halloween and Santa's elf at Christmas.

I taught Sugar how to smile and was greeted each night with her smile and kisses no matter what kind of day she had, even when congestive heart failure was causing her to cough because she was so excited to see us.

I am convinced that God gave us dogs to remind us of His unconditional love and Sugar to remind Us to strive to have unconditional for each other. Grandma certainly embodied this in her love for Glendene and me as well.

Art is the expression of the soul. This is true not only of the artist but for the subject as well. The portrait "Sugar" is the sincerest representation of her essence captured in the Glass Shard Painting.

As the morning sunlight comes in, her radiance is reflected to us as we start the day. She was a precious gift to us from God and her portrait a treasure. "Sugar" is now the finest artwork we possess.

Thank you for this precious remembrance of Sugar.

Love, Glendene and Bill and Greetings from "Sugar"

My Thoughts: A very special woman told me a lovely story regarding her request to commission me to create a GSP of a chihuahua. She introduced herself as Nancy. Nancy told me that she wanted to give dear friends a very special Christmas gift.

She explained that her friends had a chihuahua for 14 years who had passed to doggie heaven. Her name was Sugar. She was dearly loved and loved her family in return. Hearing this touched me deeply. "Thank you. I'd love to create Sugar' s likeness and beautiful soul".

I stressed the word, likeness, as I define likeness as a representation of the living soul, in this case, Sugar.

I asked Nancy to send pictures of Sugar so that I could begin the process of immortalizing Sugars' life and loves. The photos I received made me smile, especially seeing Sugars' adorable and extensive wardrobe.

My painting of Sugar contains hundreds of individually carved, shaped, and layered glass shards to create shadows and nuances which bring Sugar to life. Nancy and I worked together using facetime, and her feedback was invaluable. Sugar guided me as well. When I finally heard from Sugar that she approved of her likeness I was pleased and called Nancy on facetime so that she could see the result. Nancy said happily, "yes, that is exactly like sugar's sweet face.

I hope you are pleased, especially when you see Sugars' eyes twinkling at you every day. Namaste.

Octopus

Owner,

The Oceanographic Institute, Woods Hole, Massachusetts

Commissioned and Donated by Meg Foffonof

Living by the sea is like exploring an ever-filled jewel box. The treasures hidden under the sand and mud called to me throughout my childhood year-round promising that wonders awaited me. The first warm day in May was beach day! Bringing my pail and shovel with me, I dug continuously in the place I was sure was, The One. When the sun became too hot. I skipped over the burning sand, waiting for

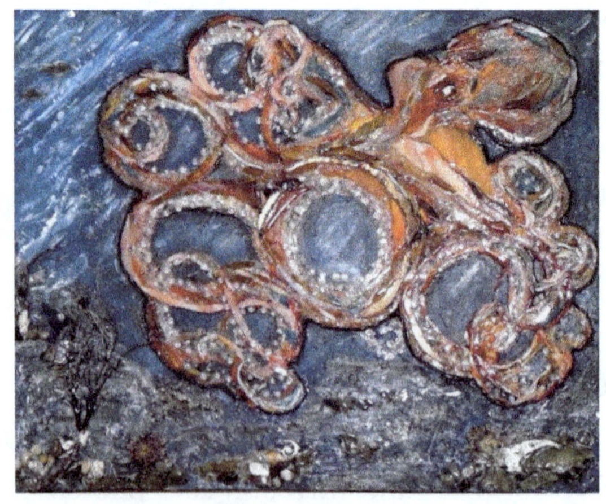

the biggest wave, jumped in and then rode back in on my belly, running to 'The Spot', believing that if I dug deep enough, I would find a baby octopus, or at least an octopus egg!

Having read stories about octopuses and seen their pictures, I knew that if I searched hard enough, one would appear, I assured my 7-year-old self.

I did not find one. My fascination with octopuses remained and when I was asked by Meg whether I could create a glass shard octopus, for the Oceanographic Institute, in Woods Hole, I unhesitatingly responded, "Of course." Above is an image of my octopus, who emerged from the reefs just as I had imagined him when I was 7 years old. See, all you must do is believe and never give up!

What follows are a few more samples of subjects and styles in my GSP portfolio. Please accept my invitation to visit more of my studio and gallery and view additional GSPs, each with their story, eager to be told.

<u>Into the Power</u>

Owner: Deborah Schechter

Deborah writes: "From the moment I saw this piece, I felt it was a personification of my best self, both physically and spiritually… full of life, erotic, a moment of energy that moved to through the world 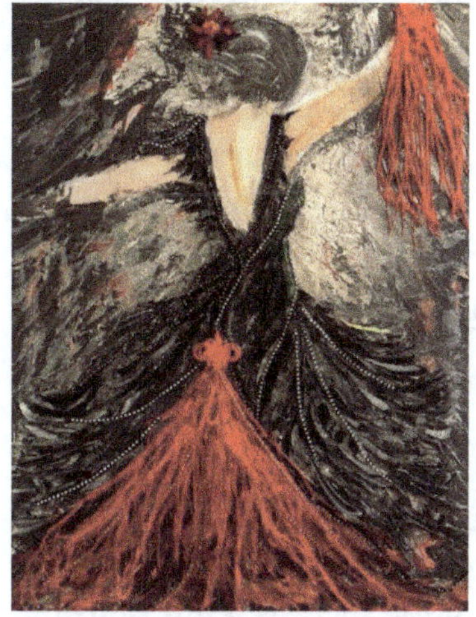 with grace and flow. I've put it on the landing of my staircase going from the first to second floor of my house, so that when I see it every day I too am in movement going up or down, breathing as I take the stairs with inhalation and exhalation that is informed by the art, infusing me with positive energy and a feeling of excitement, strength, youthful promise, going off to meet the world in all its glory.   It's whimsical and romantic, so it's mysterious and unknown, and yet has a physicality that infuses me with its passion. It brings Eleanor's spirit into mine each time I see it. It makes me happy countless times a day. Thank you, Eleanor, for this amazing creation."

My Thoughts: Into the Power was one of the first GSP where I was introduced to the magic of mixed media by my spirit guides. Painted in 2010, it was inspired by a woman who ached to leave darkness forever. The painting was a beginning. Not knowing how to go further, I left her as she was; knowing that at some time, she would be completed.

Eight years later, while passing her in the second- floor foyer, I knew that it was time to "glassify" her. A box with newly purchased beautiful iridescent black glass was in my studio. Having set it in a prominent place I "got" that this glass along with red accents and accessories was what was called for. What fun I thought, I am going to love designing this dress. (Of course, it's one I would enjoy wearing.)

A few months later, while visiting me, I mentioned to Deborah that the back of the woman reminded me of her. She stopped and said, "yes. I want it.".

What a wonderful experience to observe. Deborah is a brilliant therapist who has helped countless people break through barriers. Their collective souls had communicated that she was to be honored and recognized in this GSP. She now resides in a beautiful home in Washington, D. C. as she continues her sacred work, helping others to break through barriers where reservoirs of joy and creativity await.

I encourage you, Dear Reader, to break through whatever defenses you have created with the intention to live fully. Our life is what we create.

<u>Boss Frog</u>

Owner, Paul Robertson

In Paul's own words: "The 'Boss' occupies a central position in the sunroom of my New Hampshire lake house watching over and blessing all who pass through my home while also looking onto the pristine and tranquil waters of Conway Lake where bull frogs and Loons can be heard at night. While I was viewing Eleanor's beautiful works of art last year, the paintings of the frogs seemed to speak and connect to me. I admit I was not familiar with the symbolism of the frog at that time so upon further inquiry, learned there were multiple interpretations of frog symbolism but the ones that resonated with me was the Celtic frog as a deity over all the earth with the power to heal and purify body, mind, and spirit. The frog symbolizes Metamorphosis/Transformation and as sentient beings on earth, our lives and ability to adapt and cope depend on our willingness to accept change. In my own story so far, it has been one of change (both good and bad) and my trajectory has been one where I've had to adapt and embrace new challenges which has given me a unique perspective and insight into dealing with my fellow humans. If one is to achieve spiritual and material success, we need to recognize and embrace change to transform and enrich our existence and, on this journey, we have an important obligation to help those around us. As I continue 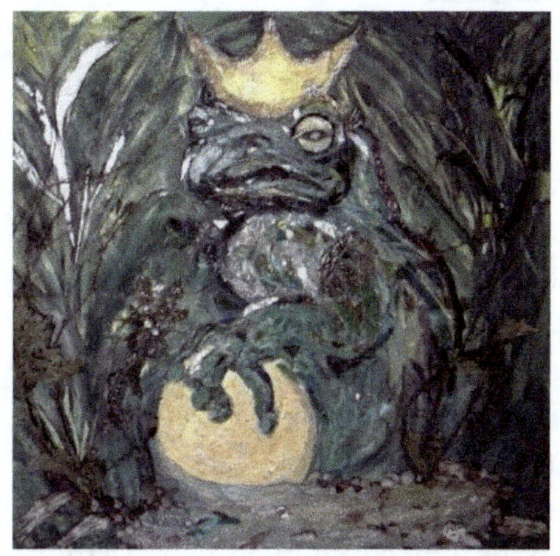 this path of healing and transformation, The Boss watches reassuringly over me as self-doubt surfaces...I look up and then out to the water of Conway Lake as my mood and confidence rises....I know my guides are never far away."

My Thoughts: My grandmother told this story as she watched me from the kitchen window when I was three years old playing in the sandbox. "You began jumping around on your hands and knees, then falling over. I came running out and saw you pointing to a frog who was jumping around your toys. You kept pointing to him saying what, what, what, what, what? I said, "frog" several times and you repeated it, except it sounded like "fwog". As the frog jumped away my grandmother said, "bye-bye frog, thank you for coming.". Before bed that night, I was introduced to Aesop's fables about frogs and my fascination with them began. As the years passed, and I began to study people in depth, I often associated them with animal characteristics.

In my GSP' s I like to create animals and capture their personalities. The idea of creating a series of frogs came to mind and the first would be the Boss Frog. Genesis says that God created people and animals on the sixth day. Boss Frog sits with his hand on the universe. He is the archetype of all frogs. His surroundings are simple, nature provides, and all is clear and simple. He is the king of this universe, exuding wisdom, peace, and tranquility.

His philosophy is, take it easy you will get there, "thy will be done."

<u>Kokopelli</u>

Owner: Jim Kircher

In his own words. "As I look at the picture of Kokopelli, I see a GSP that is amazing in every way. The picture is a classic profile of the deity vibrantly shimmering with many colors and layers of glass shards. Kokopelli has come to life! His numerous qualities and gifts served as an inspiration to several Indian nations located in the southwestern part of North America. This GSP shows him with a mischievous streak, contributing to his success as a leader of the people. It is said that wherever he went, he brought music, humor, knowledge, and wisdom to all with whom he came in contact. Among his gifts, he was a motivator and educator instructing people as to the need for agriculture and how to produce crops necessary for their existence and well-being. Under his leadership, many individuals became excellent farmers and hunters. It is also said that for over one thousand years he was considered by his people, "to be all things to all people." Other qualities defining Kokopelli were traveling salesman, warrior, and magician. Kokopelli continues to serve as a success story for a legendary life. Dr. Fisher's rendition of Kokopelli helps the legend live and inspire others to this day. With her development of Glass Shard Art, she has contributed a new definition to the word, Art. The use of multiple layers of individually carved and placed glass shards have pushed the bounds of creativity. She has captured the essence of this deity, and he has come to life. My desire is that this version of Kokopelli will live on in the Booth Western Museum in Cartersville, Georgia as the legacy of Dr. Eleanor Fisher, to continue her work and live as an inspired human being. I am personally convinced that this amazing GSP of Kokopelli will never be duplicated and will honor her and what she has accomplished in her lifetime. She has told me that if her profession as a Doctor of Psychology and an artist has in any way helped to make the world a better place to live, her life has been worthwhile."

My thoughts: Many years ago, I saw a picture of Kokopelli on a cup. Kokopelli is a Hopi word meaning (roughly) wooden backed. Most of the familiar depictions of Kokopelli are copied from Hopi art,

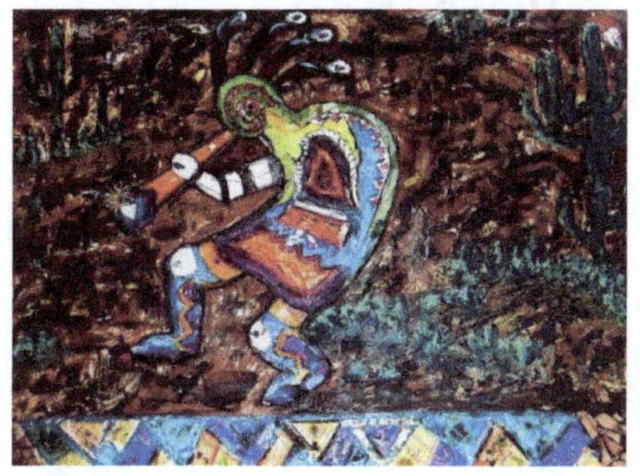

derived from ancient Anasazi glyphs. The humpbacked Flute Player is the mythical Hopi symbol of fertility, replenishment, music, dance, and mischief.

"Known as a fertility god, prankster, healer, and storyteller, he embodies the true American Southwest, and dates back over 3,000 years ago, when the first petroglyphs were carved. Although his true origins are unknown, this traveling, flute-playing Casanova is a sacred figure to many Southwestern Native Americans. Carvings of this hunch-backed flute-playing figure have been found painted and carved into rock walls and boulders throughout the Southwest."

Kokopelli's' joyful image and the tales about him have stayed with me. While traveling to several countries, including Greece, South Africa, Morocco, and Ireland, I found pieces of glass and stones, which I saved. Knowing that my work is in two categories, Fine Art and Mixed-Media, friends have brought me additional pieces which I have included to create this timeless spirit GSP.

My Little Black Dress

Owner: Maria Zuccoli

In her own words: On a lovely fall evening while attending a jazz concert at the Marblehead Arts Association, I glanced at a remarkable piece of art. Immersed in the wonderful music, I needed to wait for intermission to examine this piece. The music engaged me completely, yet, almost of its own volition, my eye kept moving towards Eleanor's GSP. Amazingly, I heard the voice of the painting speaking to me telling me, take me home!" And that is exactly what I did! This stunning ensemble is displayed over my bed. It assures me of beautiful dreams and in the morning its unique splendor stays with me and colors my day.

My Thoughts: This GSP was inspired by the idea that each woman must have a little black dress (LBD) in her wardrobe. In the 1920s Coco Chanel is said to have originated the LBD, wanting a dress that was simple and affordable. She declared: "Fashion should express the place, the moment…" and boasting that those who were not wealthy could: "walk around like millionaires. The little black dress was like a canvas that could be easily accessorized."

Agreeing completely with this, I designed my version of an LBD.

The top of the GSP shows a padded black satin hanger on which hangs a long black sheath.

Below the waist, the center is open to show a gold lame panel with its sides flared out, illustrating its fluidity. The gown features spaghetti straps and an attached train of black chiffon which can trail or be used to cover the shoulders or arms.

Opposite the chiffon scarf hangs a black beaded evening bag with diamante trim. Using iridescent black glass and carving it with undulating curves enabled the side panels to show motion and grace.

The rest of the gown uses the same black iridescent glass carved, then hand shaped to fit the bodice, straps, and evening bag. The gold panel is lame fabric, loosely fixed to the canvas, indicating motion and grace.

Towards The Sun

Owner: Rosemary Cunningham

In her own words: "I believe that we are drawn to works of art that speak to us and reflect a part of our life journey. Seeing a color, brush stroke, or pose rings a bell in my memory and I am transported

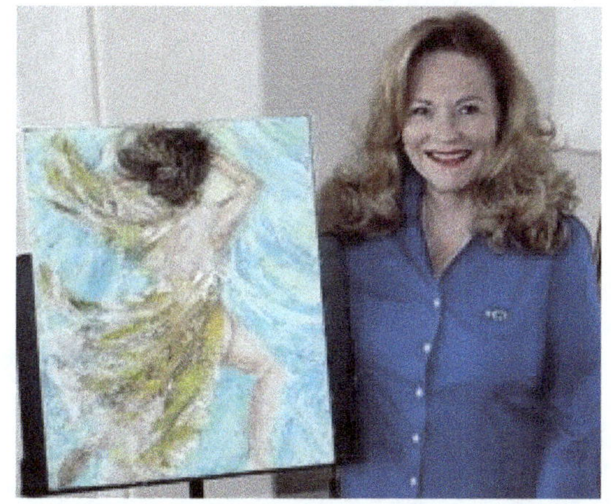

to another place. A deep shadow brings back a memory of a difficult time. I love Eleanor's GSP for its spirit and high energy. With her leap of faith, the woman has freed herself from the darkness, and moves towards the sun. Sparkling with beautiful gems in her upswept hair, she takes flight in her dress woven of gold and rays of light. She is powerful, brilliant, talented, and fearless. Residing above my "creativity chair", in my studio, she guides me, keeping me company, reminding me to keep learning, loving, and creating."

My Thoughts: This GSP was inspired by a major part of my life. Having been a therapist in full-time private practice for many years, I learned that each person has their own version of living in the dark. At the same time, each person has longed for their ideal of living in the light. Respecting the journey of individuals reinforces the knowledge that everyone does the best they can. We have our tools, not those of another.

The body of the woman in the GSP is strong, her arms are up protecting her face from the spotlights of sources which include scorn and anger for leaving the familiar darkness behind. Other bright lights are from the unaccustomed sun guiding her past unseen dangers. Her wispy dress of gold is far different than the heavy dark colors she wore before she understood and chose the concept of enlightenment. The feather boa around her shoulders, streaming out indicates the lightness which is now hers. The blue background includes soft clouds indicating infinite possibility.

Chapter Six: My Gallery, and Portfolio Samples

People often think of art galleries as large sterile rooms whose walls are filled with paintings and sculptures. My home gallery is a bit different and begins on the front porch with a display of five GSP. These are different subjects, each chosen to pique interest and welcome visitors. Inside the house, over150 GSPs, featuring a

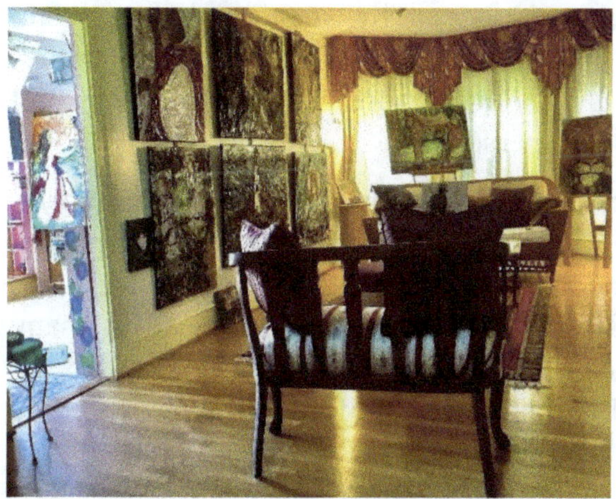

multitude of subjects, are arranged on all the walls to greet you, moving you through each room and up 2 flights of stairs.

Upstairs I do have a small, more traditional gallery for my art. It's next to the studio which is on the third floor of our old Victorian home. The picture on the left shows one view of it with the door to my studio just visible on the left. The result of all this is the fact that my home, all of it, is my gallery. That is one way my gallery differs from more traditional art galleries. The other, and to my mind the most significant difference, is no other gallery has a permanent show of glass shard paintings, unique in all the world.

In addition to their being glass shard art, another thing all my pieces have in common is they are colorful and happy, expressing my philosophy of life and love of color.

The non-traditional nature of my art is evident from the very beginning of your visit. The wide variety of subjects in glass serves to inform the guest that there is no single subject that dominates my collection. You will see women here of various cultures and historical eras, each expressing their life journey. Also included are automobiles, animals, birds, faeries, flowers, fish, and angels, to name but a few. Each GSP has a story, its history, and my reasons for its birth. I am happy to include this in writing for the new owner when a piece is purchased.

While my art is available for viewing on my website, at www.eleanorsartisticvisions.com, it is not possible to truly see them in all their reflective glory unless you see them in person. The three-dimensional qualities of GSP cannot be reproduced in two dimensions. No photograph, no matter how professionally done, can do them justice. As you move from side to side, forward and back, the light reflecting from the glass will also change, giving you so much more than a mere photo or screen image. Also, each piece evokes emotions which are better experienced by standing before them. Nevertheless, I do gratefully acknowledge the digital world and its ability to reach millions of viewers so more people can at least get some idea what they are like in person.

From the art world perspective my work fits into the categories of fine art and mixed media. But as anyone can see from my gallery or my website, I have no one favorite subject.   That said, you can find certain themes in my work.   One of these is the sea in all its many aspects. Other broad themes are animals, women, cars, and gardens. In the rest of this chapter, I will show some of my pieces and provide you with the stories behind them.

The Dancer

It is said that there are no accidents. One evening I heard the music of Ravel's Bolero. The cadence and structure of the music was hypnotic. While immersed in The Bolero, I heard the words, "complete abandonment," followed by a picture of a dancer throwing her arms over her head. I could hear the cassinettes! From beginning to end I saw and felt the erotic tension which builds, note by note until the end, sweating, out of breath, the dancer has become the crescendo.

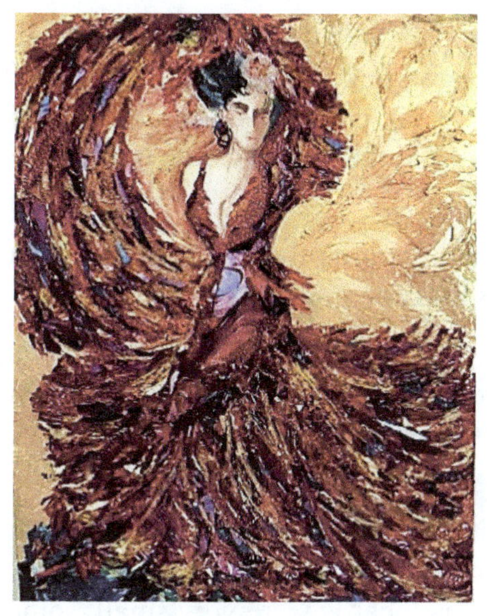

The dancer allowed us to see her moving through each plateau while experiencing the climax of the music.

The dancer, caught in that moment where she is at one with the beat of her sexuality and the music must be captured; my feelings and thoughts tumble together without an impulse to separate them. Then I heard, "passion and the ability to feel is your gift. Without passion there is no life, just glassy eyed automatons moving on a conveyor belt going through their biological and psychological lifecycles waiting to die. That is your task. Create passion; paint your life or put down your palette knives." "Ooh," I thought, "No pressure." And how long is this going to take me, I wondered. Smirking was the response I felt, returned. "You know what to do", I heard. It was clear that I could not focus on my emotions, use myself as a model and transfer personal sexuality to a new piece without assistance.

Sandra Wilmer graciously offered to pose for me again. Explaining what I wanted and guiding her she lifted her arm, lowered her head, and turned her body so that her leg was poised in the perfect position. I knew this was very tiring so after one more session, I took about a dozen photos to work from, and thanked her for her invaluable help as I continued alone.

To accurately paint 'passion' I knew the music of Bolero must be heard at the subliminal level; to be in touch with what is barely perceptible and purely emotional without my thoughts to edit and censor the baring of my soul on the canvas.

Looking at the outlines of the painting while listening to the music of the Bolero was a meditative experience and the focus was psychedelic-like as the music and the dancer merged.

Without understanding the complex steps necessary in creating the dancer, the finished picture appeared in my mind's eye. I quickly learned. The background must be simple and textured, a gold shimmer representing searing, tempering heat. This was the anchor of the painting.

Red and gold were to be the main colors; the entire medial area from the breasts through the thighs must be highlighted and honored. Many shades and textures of red and gold glass shards were carved.

Her beautiful intense face emerged, with just a few touches of a palette knife. 'don't touch it again', I heard. 'OK,' I said,' I know she's perfect'.

Bending over the canvas while applying the hundreds of glass shards was extremely tiring and I could only work 2 hours at a time. The layers of black, gold, and red glass shards were very small, some the size of my little fingernail. Some are even smaller. Many more shards needed to be carved than I anticipated; first with the diamond bladed bandsaw and then each shard hand shaped and carved with up to six cuts on each side of every piece.

Each tiny cut was needed to indicate how fast and passionate was the dancers' movements. Her gown needed to be as lush as were the final orgasmic beats of the Bolero's hypnotic rhythm.

One day while listening to "the bolero" and, polishing her thigh area with my forefinger, the music suddenly stopped. I thought the plug for the disc player had come out of the wall. It had not.

As I looked at her, my beautiful lady dancer, I knew she was present and alive. There was no more for me to do.

Mermaid Rising

Painting and "glassifying" scenes inspired by the ocean is a given since my studio and home are across the street from the Atlantic. It is 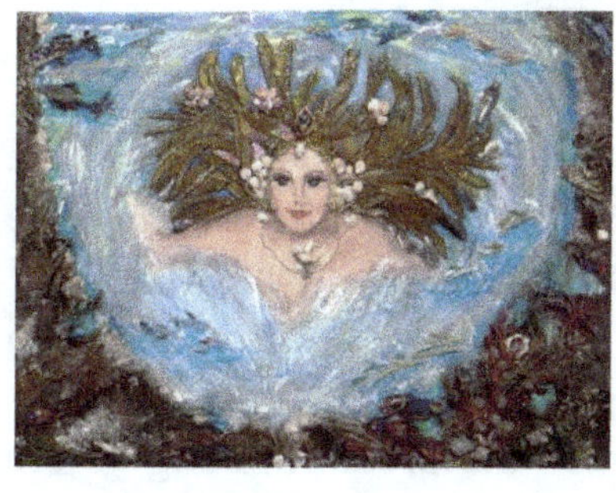 constantly changing with the seasons and with the weather and the tides and it amazes and inspires me. Gazing at the ocean, the tides coming in and out day after day, year after year, is a continuously mesmerizing experience binding me to its greatness. To see the power and majesty of nature in this way is humbling as well. How frail and inconsequential we are, indeed. It's easy for my imagination to go into the hidden realm of the sea, creating magical images of what might be there. For example, early one glorious summer morning I saw the tide was completely out. Then, I gasped, a swell of huge waves began heading to shore. At the top of the froth, a mermaid appeared seeming to look directly at me. The sun was in my eyes. I blinked, and she was gone, yet I knew I saw her, and she lives in my mind forever. This GSP is what I remember, her hair looked like coral, with pearls and shells entwined throughout and decorating her body.

Sandy

A likeness of Sandy, our Cavalier King Charles Spaniel, is on the 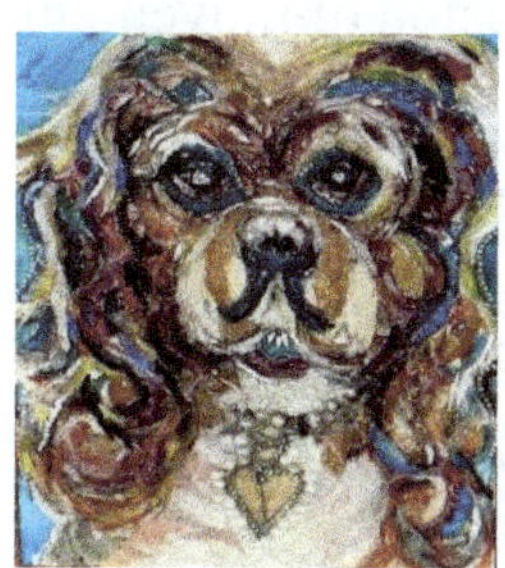 front door of our home gallery, waiting to greet and guide you as you enjoy the large display of GSP's displayed throughout the house. A major distinguishing characteristic of the Cavalier is their affectionate nature. This GSP of Sandy shows he is alert, affectionate and welcoming. His collar has his identification, along with a door sensor which operates the doggy door enabling him to come and go into our fenced yard as he pleases. It also allows him to meet and greet people at any time. The heart on his collar describes his personality and sets the tone of welcome for all who visit.

<u>Siamese Fighting Fish</u>

This GSP shows a large male Siamese Fighting Fish, also known as a Betta Fish, living under the water, among the underwater foliage and other aquatic life. At the bottom left is a rainbow lobster, showing the diversity of underwater life. Both can be found in marshes and ponds and even rice paddies in Southeast Asia. To create the colors and depths of the underwater environment the predominating colors are first chosen, then the complimentary colors; next are the other colors and mixtures to be used in creating shadows and emphasize specific elements. Finally chosen is the glass which will be carved into

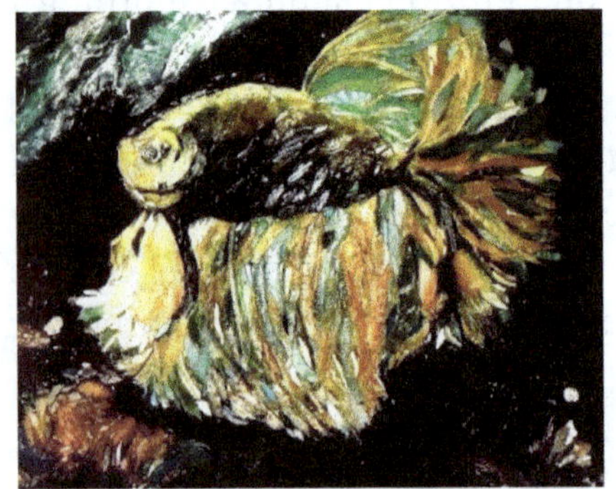

shards for the painting. Many colors and textures of glass are available as I search through the large sheets of glass or small saved glass remnants on the shelves in my studio. I search until I find just the right color and texture to achieve my vision for the finished work.

The goal is always for the finished GSP to be an authentic representation of the image as I originally conceived. Looking at the photo of this GSP you will see that most pieces of glass have several asymmetrical cuts on both sides as well as a point on each end. This creates the illusion of movement giving life to the water and the fish.

Life and movement are essential to every living thing. Every glass shard must be individually shaped, or the images would be static and lifeless. Finally, the stones and dried aquatic plant life are added to complete their underwater home.

All my work begins as a sketch on the canvas which is then painted in acrylics. When I am satisfied with the look and feel of the image, then this painted canvas becomes my template, a necessary guide, providing the foundation for the work. It is not, however, sacrosanct. While applying the glass shards sometimes my hands begin to modify the image to enhance the added medium of glass and other materials. Using iridescent glass contributes to the multidimensionality, character, and personality of the story which is included in each piece. In the image above you can see that iridescent green-turquoise colors predominate, and are noticeable throughout the fish body and fins, bringing balance to the dark waters. The fins and tail fan also contain many seemingly merged shards, layers, and colors. The pointed ends of the shards enable them to fit where I choose whether directly on the canvas or on top of the existing shards.

Color is vital to all my art and the addition of deep blue-black shards under the body creates a sense of depth and dimension. The items around the fish, vegetation, other sea creatures and air bubbles, are important additions providing a glimpse of life in this watery environment.

<u>Father And Son</u>

Bettas often eat their young, but my goal in this GSP was to show the love of a father for his son. The little fish is a boy since his plumage and colors are bright, unlike the duller colors of the females. The father looks out for predators and swims, fins spread fully, providing shelter and protection for his son. He is poised at the ready position.

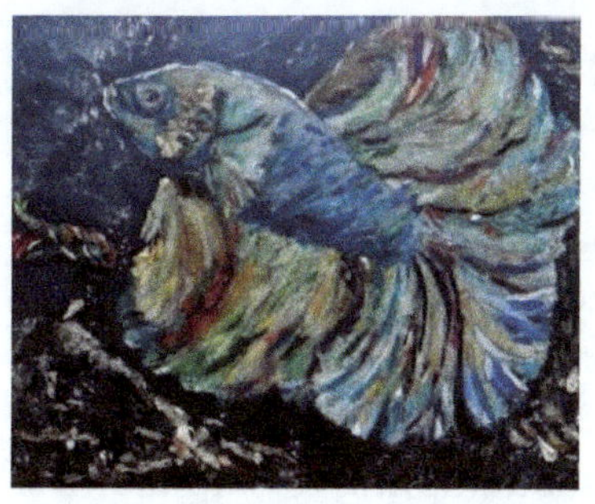

Creating the small male betta was a very time-consuming task, requiring each shard be carved about the size of my small fingernail. It took many hours to do this since the little boy fish also is alive. Additionally, the details include shadows, subtleties of color, dimension, and placement to demonstrate the connection between father and son. As I was thinking about this story, the thought came to mind of a loving father introducing his little son to the pleasures of the water, watching out for him, letting him play, and seeing that he is not hurt or in danger. The diverse vegetation, fish of every variety, present the same issues as life anywhere with all its attractions, pleasures, detours, and dangers to be navigated. The ground under the water, with its innumerable rocks and nooks and crannies provides homes and shelters to friend and foe alike.

<u>Portal</u>

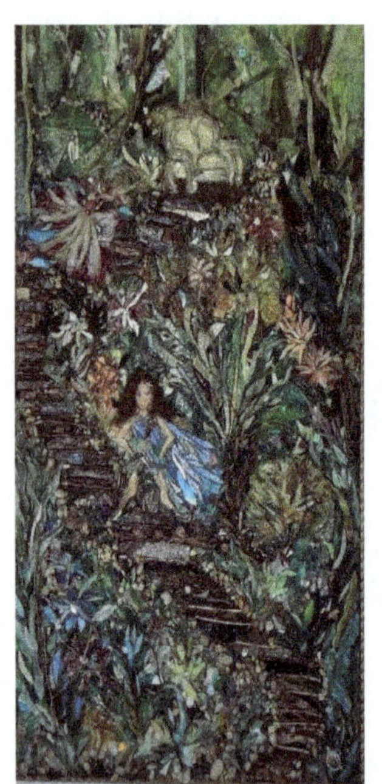

"Portal," faces the garden and the sea; each with elements that are life-giving and enhancing. This GSP highlights milestones in every life's journey. Metaphorically, many essential life issues are represented throughout the visual narrative. The size of the canvas led me to wonder what a 5-foot high by two ½ feet wide canvas could say. This was one of my earliest paintings, a part of the family of 'teaching myself to paint'. This was during the early days of smashing glass with a big iron mallet on a large paving stone, long before I knew about wet-saws and glass nippers. Many of my GSPs feature stairs and various levels. In Portal, as well as others, they indicate attitudes, behaviors, and levels of consciousness in life's journey.

There are two very distinct levels, with definite markers. I do not think there is such a thing in navigating life as 'the easy-way' unless you understand the 'easy- way' is doing it the right way, where focus, concentration, and patience constitute the stairway to success. Far fewer errors occur as I practice this moral template. Shortcuts are effective only when the path is familiar, having previously done it successfully. At the bottom right of the picture is a turtle trying to get up the stairs, attempting to skip the first two levels. There is a large stone blocking his way and he will find, no matter his efforts, he must go back to the beginning. This underscores the fact that shortcuts in life rarely give the 'breakthrough' they imagined for themselves.

About one-third of the way up the stairs, an angel stands with one question to ask and to be answered. That is, 'have you walked your talk.'? If you say yes, further questions are asked to make sure you told the truth. If you have been honorable, having owned your mistakes and learned from them, you go ahead up the stairs. At the next level, a butterfly flutters, a symbol for metamorphosis. An entirely different realm awaits above where sight is clearer, and mundane babble does not exist. When ready, advancement is to the chair of wisdom and meditation, where the realm of infinite possibility resides.

A few years ago, I decided to remake this GSP knowing that the process would take about three months. Intending to enhance the messages just described, I carved all new shards, layering them on top of the original ones. The story of portal appeared refreshed, engaging, with even more of a beating pulse.

<u>Winston</u>

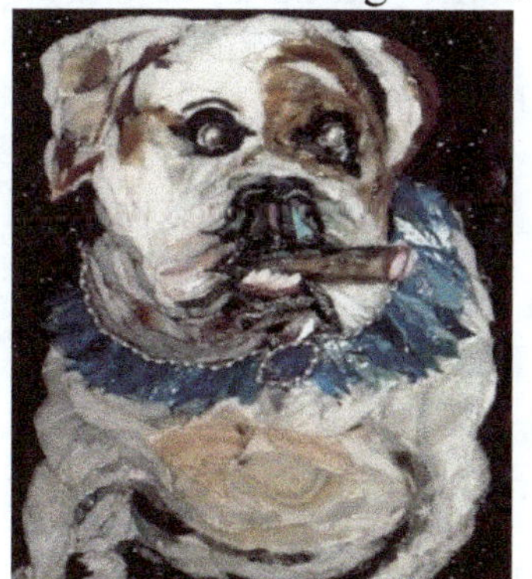

On the inner foyer door, a white bulldog greets you as he continues chewing on his cigar. He lives in the next town. While he was walking with his siblings, I saw them and thought they were adorable, then asked his dad if I could take his photo. Looking at the photos of the family of bulldogs sitting complacently on the sidewalk, I could see Winston's delightful personality, with a hint of hidden mischief shining through, and I could hardly wait to capture his likeness on canvas as a GSP. When his image was complete, I realized more was needed. With that I heard, 'close your eyes and visualize a collar'. There he appeared; this collar was around his neck and the cigar hanging out of his mouth on his left side. He named himself Winston.

'57 Chevy Surfer

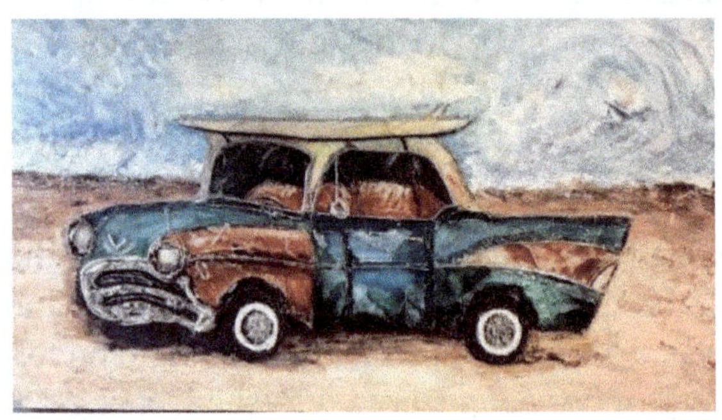

Just inside the front door, on the right, is my '57 Chevy with a surfboard on its roof. It's an iconic car reminiscent of the great times at the beach in the 50s and 60s. The music was blasting; with Elvis, Chubby Checker, and the Beach Boys doing their thing. Seems nobody could sit still in this time of innocence. The car is now rusty in spots, yet with imagination and parts recovered from the junkyard, lots of elbow grease, and enthusiasm it remains a Wow ride. A vehicle for fun!

This painting came about after I said to my husband one day "I can't think of anything new to paint, any ideas?" Followed by, "I'm looking for something completely different that I've never done and know nothing about. He responded, "Why don't you do a '57 chevy with a surfboard on top, they're iconic!" I replied, 'The only thing I know about cars is make sure there is plenty of gas and lock it, and don't forget the keys when I get out." He laughed and said, "You can do it."

Trusting his judgment, I said, "OK, that should be fun.". Then, to myself, 'How am I going to do that?' Once again, brand new project! My desire for a challenge came to the fore, my search to learn is ongoing, never-ending, how to do it better, make it come alive.

With my husband's assurance that the 1957 Chevrolet Belaire was an iconic automobile which would be an interesting and challenging subject, I began my research. The definition of icon is a person or thing regarded as a representative symbol instantly recognized around the world. Almost every article stated that the 1957 Chevy is indeed one of America's most iconic images. Various articles explained why it was an icon; it included every major styling element from a decade characterized by the outlandish. In 1957, Chevrolet's quality was much better than the competition. So, the '57 Chevy was well-liked when new, and later, as late-model or even now antique used cars. They looked great, were mechanically sound, took abuse well, and when they did break, they weren't expensive to fix. The '57 Chevy has also been a popular toy in plastic as well as something to display on one's desk. It can sometimes be seen as a kit for go-carts or other recreation vehicles. Pictures of it, often in its popular turquoise paint with white fins, can be seen everywhere men work on cars. I enjoy seeing them at local antique automobile rallies and shows.

I remembered owning a '57 Chevy and my pleasure driving it. It felt sporty, had bright white fins which were not rusty, and the fenders matched each other. When it was new or used before, I bought it, no doubt countless other people had enjoyed driving it, and being seen in it. The idea of some rust spots and a slightly dented grille still giving pleasure to others was appealing. My interpretation is about the fun others have today, whether rusted or in perfect condition. This Glass Shard Painting is therefore a testament to its long-lasting value, and its storied past. Growing up in New England, I learned the expression of, "don't throw it out, find other uses for it!"

Moving into the main foyer of our home about twenty other GSP's of varying sizes and subjects are arranged on the walls. With more than 130 paintings displayed in different rooms, on different floors, each one seems to reach out saying, do not hurry, there is lots to see and experience. I hope you enjoy seeing the sample of my paintings shown below.

Marblehead Jazz

The GSP called Marblehead Jazz often sits on a large easel in the main foyer, welcoming you to the concert. It took me a year to complete this. Never having played an instrument, much less in a 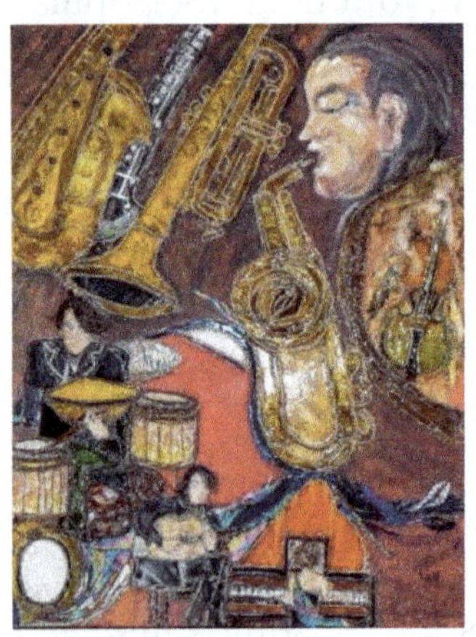 band, a lot of research was necessary to create a balanced musical scene which included artists playing their instruments, immersed in their music. My purpose was to honor and recognize the pleasure musicians add to our lives.

The Marblehead Arts Association, of which I am a juried artist member, hosts wonderful concerts which my husband and I are keen to attend. Sitting in the front row, I took many photographs over a three-month period to capture these artists whose playing invited us into their mesmerizing music.

Eager to begin transferring my photographs onto canvas, I began developing the painting so that the proportions would be correct and balanced. Since the GSP features five artists, their instruments, and many small and large elements, the process along with the initial sketching took about a week. I took care that each instrument and musician would be featured appropriately, and that the entire story would be compelling.

For instance, the woman playing the cello is positioned at the shoulder of the musician playing the saxophone at the top right. Except for him, all the figures have real hair. Their hair seems to move as they play their instruments, completely immersed in the music which leads them.

Icons of Boston

This GSP represents the many iconic, historic sites in Boston. Growing up just 10 miles north and commuting daily to college in the city, which Bostonians lovingly call "The Hub of the Universe", or simply "The Hub" was a major influence in my life. This painting is my homage to the historic landmarks from this marvelous city; the CITGO sign at Fenway Park, home of the beloved Boston Red Socks, The Old North Church, where the lanterns were hung to warn the people of the British invasion: "One if by land, two if by sea," the Prudential Center with its famous observation room at the top, giving

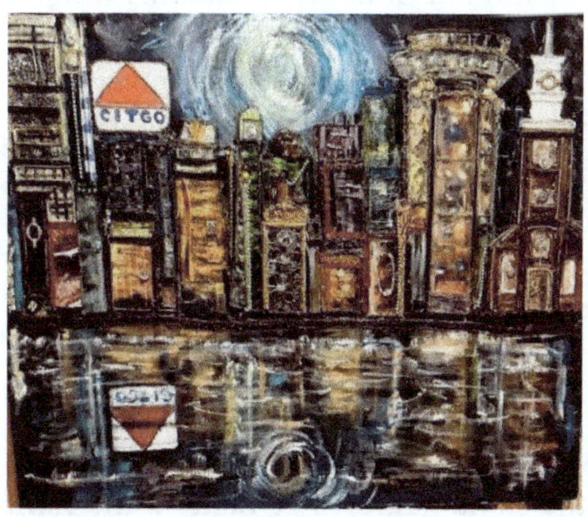

a tremendous view of the city and Boston Harbor. And of course in the foreground we see the Charles River. Anyone who has been there knows that you can't see all these icons at the same time, owing to their actual locations in the city, but I captured them here in a fanciful way to highlight them together, and reflected in the Charles. This GSP is my love letter to my home, every aspect a bookmark in my life. Visitors to Boston explore the streets, tracing the steps of Paul Revere and other historic figures and events. The area downtown where once the waterfront began, is the inspiration for icons of Boston. Walking along these streets, going to restaurants, theater, or shopping, giving directions to people from other countries enabled me to chat with them, to briefly make their acquaintance, and welcome them to our city. The streets, buildings, waterfront and Harbor Islands all have unique stories to tell. I think of my life and visits to these places and appreciate all who I have met there.

Red Sky in the Morning

One morning, glancing out my studio window, I was stunned,

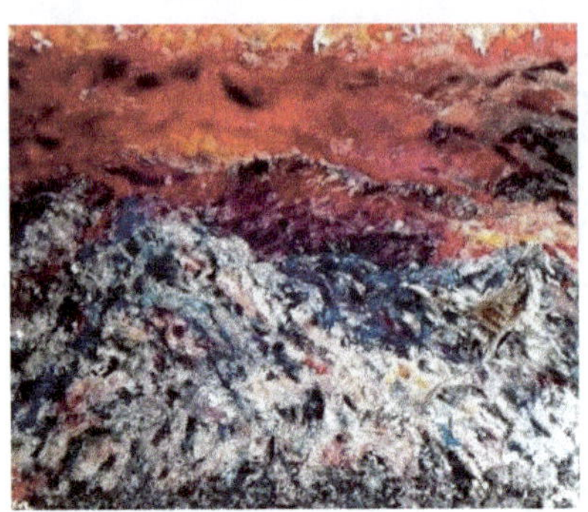

watching this scene unfold. I stood transfixed, then grabbed my camera, ran up the stairs to the roof deck and started clicking. What an extraordinary scene! I still have a hard time describing what I saw and doing it justice. It was as if I had been infused with seeing and feeling the essence of intense passion, some vision out of history. Looking out my large dormer window in my studio, the storm raged over the seawall, the white waves kept rolling and angrily crashing straight up over twenty feet soaking the awe-struck crowds of people buffeted by the uncontrollable sea. There was no doubt, I must create a GSP entitled, "Red Sky in the Morning," Living across the street from the Atlantic Ocean, I have witnessed the scene unfold many times, especially in the winter. A nor'easter inundating and pounding Red Rock is majestic to behold!

The left side of this GSP shows the Red Rock, a timeless, unassailable edifice in Lynn, MA, repeatedly slammed by the angry sea, flanked by a state park of the same name. The boat on the right is lifted, carried, and broken in pieces which are then carried away. The other side shows a large fish, appearing to jump high, yet tossed from the deep as debris. The seagulls can be seen, cawing their distress, frantically seeking shelter from this devastation.

Being in the presence of this show of ultimate power clearly demonstrates the fragility of human beings. The huge waves roll in and then, bang! The water crashes relentlessly over the seawall while astonished onlookers stand as if hypnotized and are often drenched in the process.

Over there, a person standing on a rock is unaware aware of the danger and is thrown out to sea while others, frozen in place, watch in horror. The violent suddenness of the sea makes saving anyone impossible. All we have left is our indelible memories.

For you to see Red Sky and feel its force and majesty, with many layers and colors of glass shards, depicting the violence of the ocean is a moving experience. The rocks, pebbles, and seashells are included to add reality to the overall vision. All these elements are necessary to experience this moment in time. Feel the cold, wet wind blowing so hard you can barely stand! Only with moments such as these do we see how insignificant we are, and that indeed it is nature who controls everything.

<u>Ruby Fish</u>

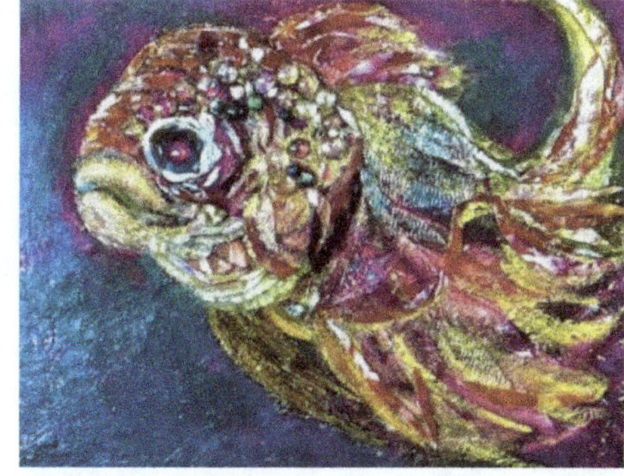

Growing up by the Atlantic Ocean fish of all sorts were a regular part of my family's menu. A treasured childhood memory was of early morning fishing trips to Gloucester with my dad. I was 10 years old, and he baited my drop line with a wriggling worm, and I caught a 52 -pound cod. (He pulled it up)

A visit to China presented opportunities to sample unfamiliar varieties of fish; their freshness, preparation and regional herbs resulted in brand-new wonderful flavors. After returning in mid-October, I knew winter was around the corner, hearing that a nor'easter was set to pound us, earlier than usual.

I recalled the wonderful fish eaten in China and the idea of painting a fish came to mind. "Never done that before." I thought and heard, "what are you waiting for? "Ok, leave me alone" I responded, "I'll do it; all I know is how to cook fish, and how to remove the bones."

A large, detailed color wheel is on a wall in my studio. It seemed that the gold tones and jewel like compliments were flashing, indicating what would create delectable colors. Next appeared a rainbow finned fish with sparkling red eyes. Wow, that sounded like fun; it's me, I am a rainbow fish with glowing red eyes. "Why not" I heard and began to create his story, what he would look like, personality, and his job.

Beginning to sketch, the eyes and body seem to come easily. However, I could only think of saying smile to create a happy fish. The large eyes seemed to come easily as did the body. However, I'd never seen a happy fish, so I thought, smile, and what emerged was a happy boy fish with punky hair combed to the back of his head. He liked to frolic and was the leader of his shoal.

When choosing the colors for his body I imagined luscious ripe mangoes, yellow pears, delicious cantaloupes. The application of the paint and glass shards needed to proclaim that he was adorable and brave. I knew the glass shard carving would be difficult since numerous layers are needed to create the iridescent scales, their movement and the shadows indicating the anatomy under the glowing skin. Additionally, he must convey that he is happily and playfully at home.

St. Johns, British Virgin Islands, and the undersea coral gardens is a perfect place for snorkeling. Recalling the first time exploring the reefs, I remembered a visceral connection to the multicolored rainbow-like fish.

Looking at my photos of this magical place, and remembering the experience inspired me to create my smiling fish with his sparkling red eyes.

He lives there along with the dolphins and other creatures in this paradise.

A Day on the Bay

My life just north of Boston has always been influenced by the sea. Inhaling the familiar salty brine surrounded by boats of all shapes and sizes left indelible impressions on my thinking. The ocean's intense colors, challenges, majesty, and absolute power are burned

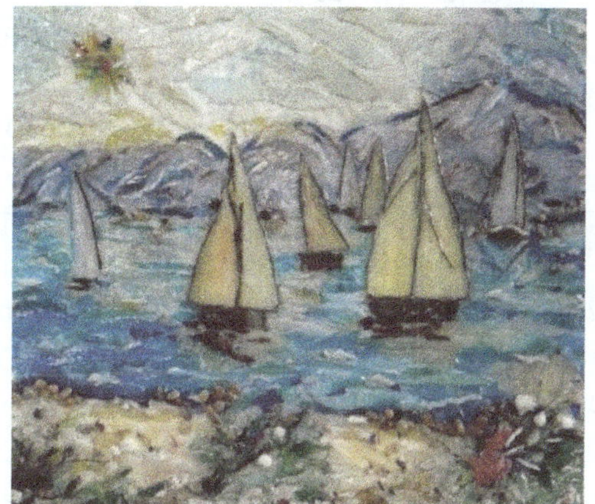

irrevocably into my brain. The fishing boats, yachts, sailors, and rowboats have the commonality of survival and victory. Lives always against the elements; never a doubt as sheets with full masts, racing, all crew as one body and mind.

My GSP "A Day on the Bay" captures the perfect sailing day with each boat showing its best as it prepares to merge with the waves bringing the crew victory. Using twigs from my garden, stones, and seashells from the beach, a sense of oneness enfolds the viewer through a spiritual connection to the sea.

The Flower Shop

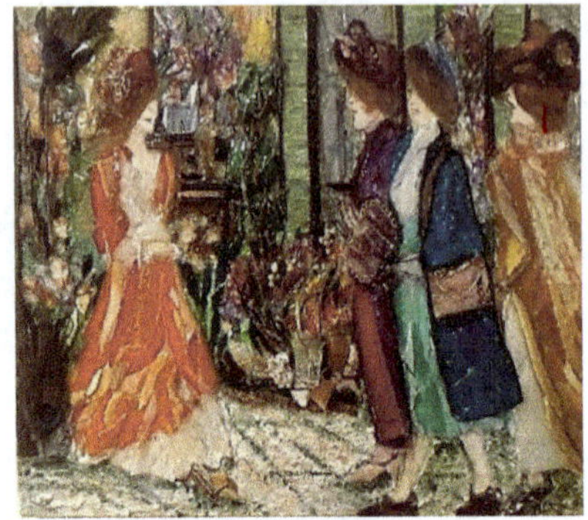

The Flower Shop provides an instructive glimpse into the design elements typical of my GSPs. On its face it shows a slice of life representing one of the struggles people have; "Will they talk to me, or will I be rejected? Will I connect to others or be shunned?" Each woman has her story. Do they care about anyone else besides themselves? The clothes and setting are the 1940s. It is particularly interesting for me to research this era, so close to mine, and remember pictures of how my mother looked and what she wore. As I design the clothes, hairstyles, hats, shoes, jewelry, and accessories, memories, and pictures of me playing in her closet come flooding to my mind.

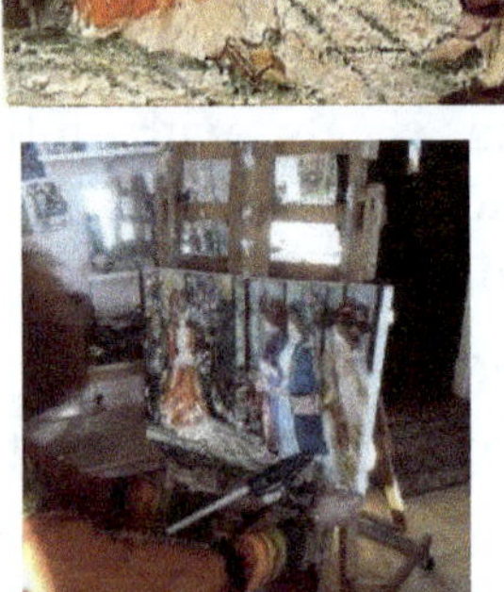

The similarities and differences between the clothes then and now are obvious. It can be fun and appealing to be able to dress the way our relatives did, especially since many of them are still with us.

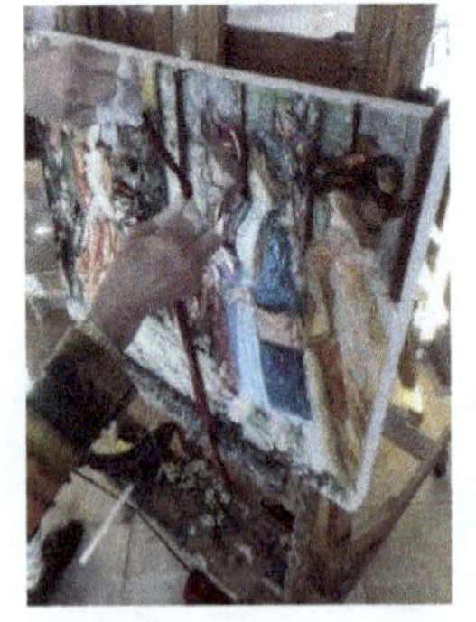

The major finishing element used in the flower shop is thin embossed brown braid. The photos below are an example of how I do this. The completed picture may be studied to see the braid's integration. My fingers are protected using latex covers, made necessary because the high heat of the hot glue drips on my finger. I also wear an apron to protect my clothing. Top photo on the left shows me using the hot glue gun to adhere the trim to the blue shoulder bag. The trim is extremely useful in separating various design elements to emphasize areas of importance.

Dawn at Nahant Lifeboat Station

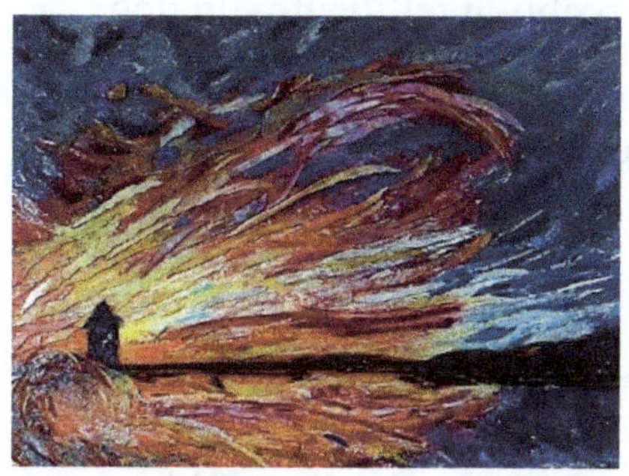

This GSP is my emotional interpretation of dawn in a specific place at a specific time. The painted canvas is my template, a necessary guide, providing the foundation, however not an absolute. The photograph here shows where I have added the colored glass shards using the painting as my guide. Historically, safe ocean travel was in large part due to lighthouses which guided our ships and crews safely home. One freezing cold, early morning, at the end of March while having breakfast, I turned my head and saw dawn with its kaleidoscope of colors rising over the horizon reflecting in the sea below. Wearing nothing over my bathrobe, I grabbed my camera and ran up three flights of stairs to my studio, up another twenty stairs to the large roof deck on top of my home. Watching the sunrise over the sea was a magnificent sight to behold. To add a point of interest, I painted the profile of the Nahant lifeboat station's tower. This design element was in part an homage to my years in the US Coast Guard Auxiliary.

Mount Kilimanjaro

This GSP was inspired by a camera Safari to Kenya and Tanzania. This was my second trip and I eagerly looked forward to introducing my husband to the spectacular experiences of visiting the animals in their natural, daily habitat. Serengeti National Park in the north of Tanzania, is 5, 700 square miles on Africa's eastern coast. We explored the Ngorongoro Conservation Area, 3,200 square miles of protected land suitable for wild animal observation.

Some of the animals we saw were remarkably close to us in our open four to six passenger jeep (that means no protection from the animals) just the canvas top to protect against the sun's rays. There was, fortunately, a guide sitting on a seat on the hood holding a loaded rifle. We saw and photographed lions, a pregnant leopard in a tree,

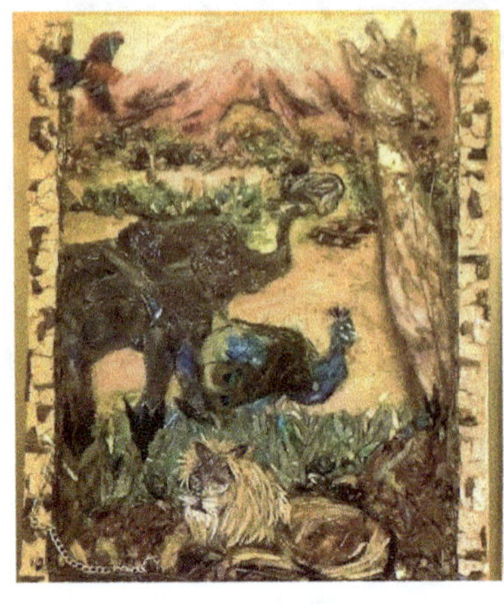

giraffes in packs, water buffalo, gazelles, kudu, and tracked the packs of remarkably intelligent wild dogs.

Mount Kilimanjaro, featured prominently in this GSP is a volcanic mountain located in Tanzania, East Africa. Also popularly known as the Roof of Africa, the gigantic sight measures 5,895 meters or 19,340 feet above sea level. It is the largest free-standing mountain in the world.

Most memorable were the animals who live together in the same park almost as if they work cooperatively. Predator and prey together; fascinating! While watching and photographing all this, I knew that I would attempt to create the magnificence of the animals and tell their story relating it to our lives.

I framed the scene in travertine marble with its beautiful coloring and rough texture. My blocks of travertine marble are about 6 inches deep necessitating the use of my tile saw to cut slice the marble down to ¼ of an inch thick. On the interior surface of the image, I scattered pieces of brown stone, representing the surface of the Ngorongoro and on the interior of the gate, I applied a vertical strip of deep brown glass, adding visual distance to the scene.

Mount Kilimanjaro is in the background with snow on its top and with rivulets, crevices, and tracks which are often used by climbers. I created Mount Kilimanjaro through texturing and then using my heat gun to raise surfaces in a pattern. Continuing to its base, mountains and hillocks are indicated along with the vegetation. Top left a colorful bird is flying, feeling safe, ready to explore the area. Meandering is a hippo, a giraffe looking out, and an elephant walking, accompanied by a male peacock.

At the bottom a lion is dozing, occasionally looking around as he relaxes on the cliff, overlooking his kingdom. Next to him, is a chain, unlocked, and hanging down at the side. In the fantasy I created all the animals came together and decided they would prefer to live peacefully together as the growing number of chain link fences curtail their ability to move freely over the vast plains. The chain had been in place to prevent the lion from terrorizing the other inhabitants but is no longer needed as fear has left and living cooperatively reigns in the animal kingdom.

Fabulous Undersea Garden

My husband Dennis named this GSP the Fabulous Undersea Garden. I tell people this is the 'real' story of how baby fish are born, pointing out the stork shaped shell positioned and gestating, top left.

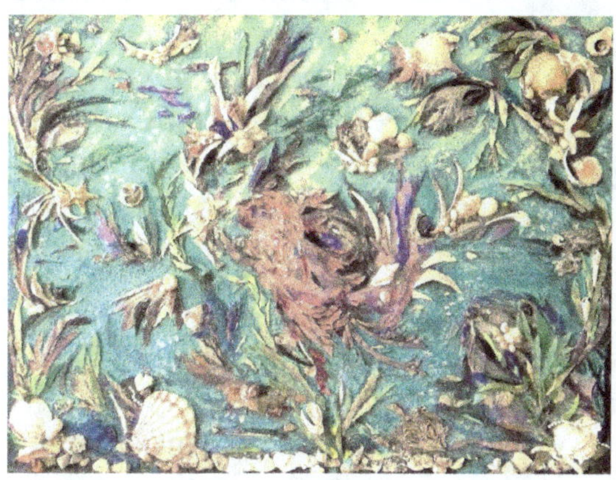

After deciding that the theme was the story of birth in the garden under the sea, I painted and textured the background in turquoise with light coming from the surface above. Next in the center some chunks of iridescent bright pink glass appeared which inspired me to create a birdfish. Since I often create my own species, birthing a birdfish was not a surprise. A Birdfish became the centerpiece, reigning majestically with iridescent pink fins glowing. Usually, I only have a general idea of the finished picture as each glass shard seems drawn magnetically to another, creating itself.

Who Is In the Mirror

The subject of this GSP is, "I wish I was someone else. Who am I and what am I?" These are questions which have always been asked

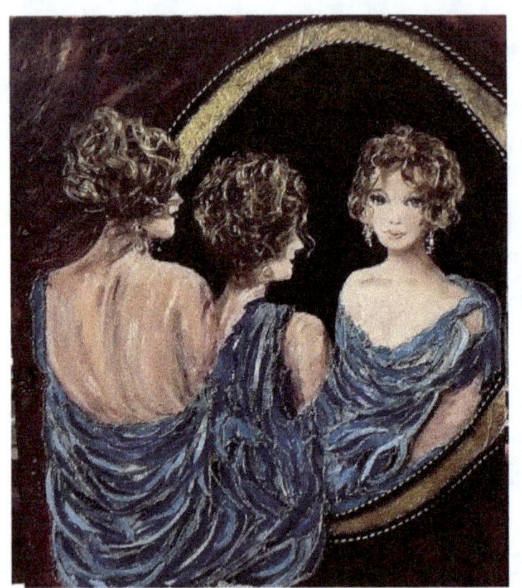

by everyone at some time in their lives. Hearing someone say to me, "I wish I was just like you," caused me to think what that would look like in a GSP. We create ideals to torture ourselves that we are not as good as some other person we know. Sitting comfortably in front of a mirror a woman looks out, eyes to the side. Does she see a memory of the past and the price of attempting to be somebody else other than herself?

Without consideration, these two other women have chosen to give their identity away in favor of becoming an idolized image in an elaborate frame – the reflection in the mirror. They have merged. Their individuality, extinguished. One figure has already begun climbing into the mirror to become someone else. Is there a lesson here of perpetual dissatisfaction?

I Choose Freedom!

This picture is a departure from my usual "light, colorful, and fun" subjects. It is darker because it deals with a much darker subject than a flower garden or other colorful thing. This GSP was inspired by a visit to Pula, Croatia. The immense Roman colosseum there is the major attraction of the city, and we entered the arena's lower levels through huge iron doors walking on uneven large stone stairs which seemed to go on forever. In its day, the arena hosted throngs of people

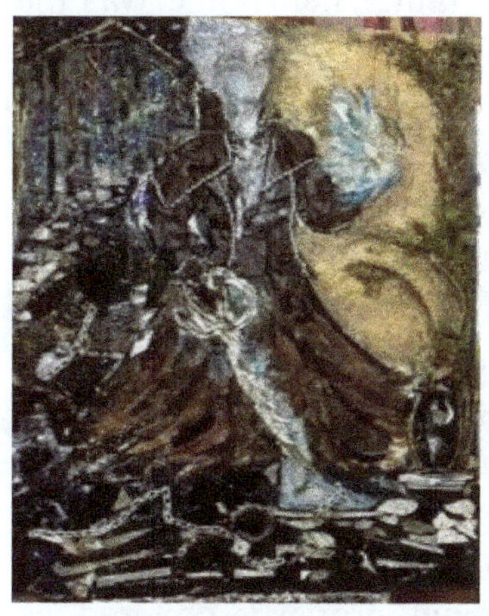

to see the gladiator slaves fight one another, sometimes to the death. They used all manner of weapons, including bare fists, nets, knives, swords, or other weapons. The purpose of the battles was to entertain the population, much like the sport competitions of our time. For the gladiators it was simple. You fought for your life. The winner lived and could even be freed. No wounded existed; they died, often bleeding to death while the crowds impatiently waited for the next round of entertainment. Under the arena we were shown the stalls where men and women slaves were kept. They were chained unless they were used as objects for the soldiers to practice on or brought to the arena as entertainment to be tortured.

Remnants of wine and olive pressing, grinding grains into flour and bakeries also existed in the adjacent area as well as olive oil presses and the large amphoras which were used for storage.

The horrific situation described to us by the tour guide caused me to create this GSP in honor of the women who rebelled, removed their chains, escaped with bare feet, ending their imprisonment, and choosing freedom, even if it meant their death. In my GSP I left a small amount of broken chain around her ankle. A piece of her chain was placed around her throat as her necklace. When all women say, "I own myself," the necklace will be removed.

Welcome to My Home

This GSP was created to represent the original owners of my home and their lifestyles. The house was built in 1891, near the end of the very stiff Victorian era. This was the "Golden Age" of optimism and less formal lives, taking people into a new millennium with its new fashions and architecture and art nouveau. In my mind the lady

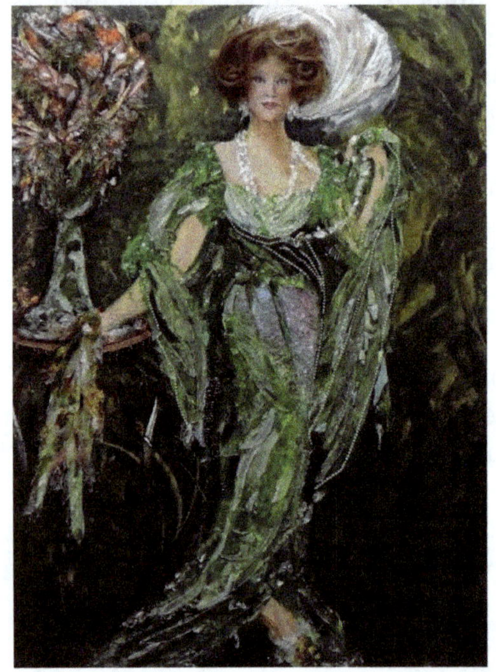

of the house would have been graceful and elegant, and she and her husband would often entertain. Their home was the centerpiece of the estate, with its Porte Cochere protecting guests from the weather as they entered and left. A wraparound porch was considered the ultimate for its time and much entertainment was enjoyed there as well. Inside the property, a magnificent garden flourished from spring into fall. The original property covered an entire block and sloped gently to the ocean. As I first approached this house in January 1981, my heart began to beat a little faster. The area, the street, and the house seemed familiar. I walked into each of the fifteen rooms, then explored the cellar and the attic. Next, walking out on the front porch, unhesitatingly I told the realtor, "I will take it." Moving in day was April 1, 1981. When I bought the house, it was surrounded with overgrown bushes and weeds. Remembering my childhood vow of having a beautiful garden, I cleared the hedges, installed a solid, six-foot wooden fence around the entire property and began to bring my dream to life in 1985. It has a personality, and its mood is whimsical, featuring a fishpond, and waterfall, trees, flowers, fruits vegetables, herbs and varied somewhat quirky statuary and artifacts. The soil is rich and friable, welcoming all which is planted. The view of the ocean from the studio window facing East is unparalleled.

Sometimes, while sleeping, my dreams show me how happy I am to be back here, in my home which I love. I am safe. I walk around the familiar rooms feeling all the history and love that has been here since the house was built a century earlier.

Today, my art gallery consisting of more than 130 GSP, begins on the wraparound porch, where six pictures are displayed. This display extends to every wall in the house and up thirty-two stairs to my studio. Entering the third floor, a long comfortable gallery with seating for 7 is available.

At one time, my studio on the third floor was the servants' quarters. As I worked, listening to the image, the woman in the painting began to appear.

On completion, it was hung in a prominent place at the top of the stairway, entering the third-floor gallery. When people view this GSP almost every comment I hear includes, either "that's you, or what a great self-portrait, followed by, "Is that your actual hair?"

Because I am self-taught, many of the women's faces have some resemblance to me. While painting women, I keep looking in the mirror checking the shape of the face, features, and body proportions. The idea of a self-portrait was not my intention and never occurred to me.

<u>Archangel</u>

The GSP of Archangel was inspired as I dreamt about being strong enough to fly. While sleeping I heard myself say "What would that take"? The answer was immediate, flying meant enlightenment; letting go of daily self-imposed burdens and stresses, including the backbreaking work of obligations to others; never asked for, never expected. Weights added upon shoulders, so heavy. Eventually forward movement slows down to a crawl, hoping for grateful

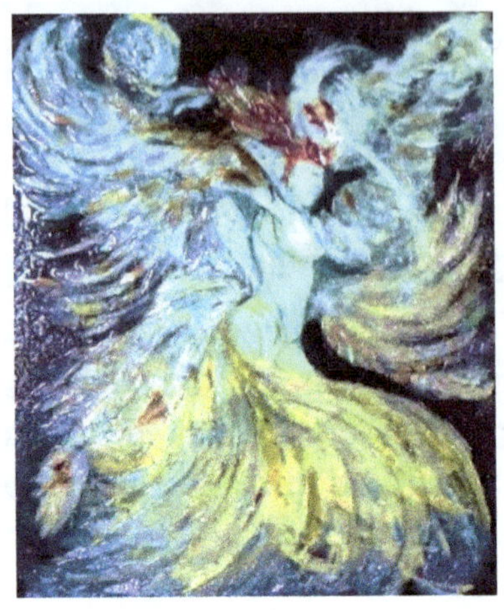

supplicants to come and appreciate, followed by the projection of perfection to follow.

Archangel defines a woman of strength, intention, and self-determination. I heard from my guides, "She represents all women demonstrating that, as she chooses, so she lives."

<u>Cecil the Lion</u>

My husband and I love to travel. On a trip to south Africa, we enjoyed a camera safari through different game parks. We saw the "big five" in the first three days! These are lions, leopards, rhinos, elephants, and cape buffalo. We saw many more aside from them and the magnificence included the scenery, interaction with people, seeing, tracking, and photographing the animals so close to our jeep.

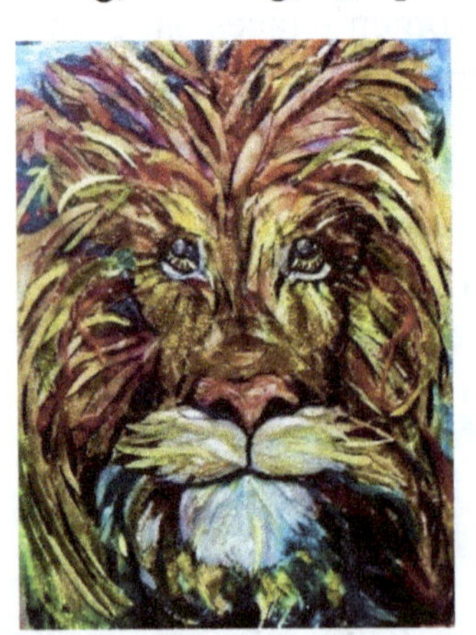

I took many pictures of the animals in their habitat. Some of the extraordinary photos were of male lions eating their kill before allowing the lionesses to feed, even though it was them who brought that kill down. Lionesses wait until the males are through and then eat what is left. The GSP pictured here was inspired by these experiences and the tragedy of his untimely death. His name was Cecil. It feels to me that this likeness represents his majesty. This GSP is in his everlasting memory and honor. He was killed as a trophy by a hunter several years ago.

<u>Make A Joyful Noise</u>

This GSP was inspired by the whirling dervish dancers, I saw in Turkey. The moment they began to dance, they became one with the music, its beat, tempo, and history. Many dances have similar

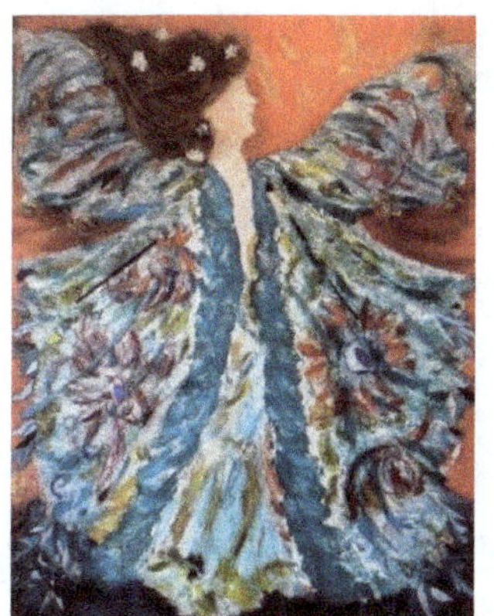

movements; to me, theirs is incomparable. Mesmerized, I dreamt about a woman in ecstasy dancing to the music that she understood, completely oblivious except for what she was hearing; each note conveying her further into another realm. A transpersonal journey moves you from your physical body to the sensory state, the dancer and the music become one.

After experiencing ecstasy, it is not possible to continue as if bliss had not been experienced. The mundane is no longer acceptable. Ecstasy is the goal.

<u>My Magical Horse</u>

People have asked why I haven't painted horses. My response has been, 'I know nothing about the anatomy of horses, how would I begin?" During a dream, I heard, 'you've learned enough, now, go paint horses, we will guide you'.

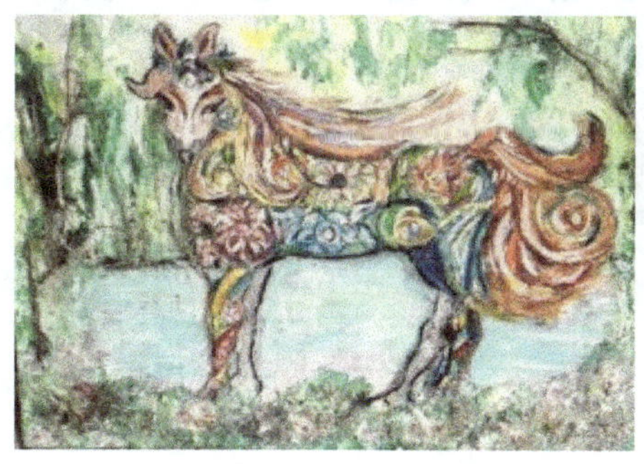

The next morning, I spotted an old photo on my kitchen wall of a picture of me on a horse that I had ridden. Quickly, I sketched a horse with a background resembling my garden. I thought I would copy the horse in the photo. I was wrong. I began painting and designing and my beautiful magical horse emerged on the canvas.

He is included in my series of three different horses. His colors are bright, and the flowers are jewel-like as are his sparkling eyes. His bridle is adorned with gold and diamond chains as befits his purpose.

It is common to have wishes about being able to go anywhere you desire. Countless songs, stories, and poems have been written about this longing. It is possible to have this wish come true while sitting atop My Magical Horse.

<u>Genesis</u>

This GSP is my final picture here. The name Genesis means birth or the beginning of everything. Genesis is represented in the center of the piece by the smallest chip of the rarest Ruby that is barely discernible. It is surrounded by a nest of ethereal diamonds. The diamonds are the womb, and the ruby is the fetus before birth. All that is needed is given to everyone. Birth occurs and the journey begins then continues. I have called this process of GSP development, parenting, as each GSP has had a period of gestation, labor, birth, and adoption.

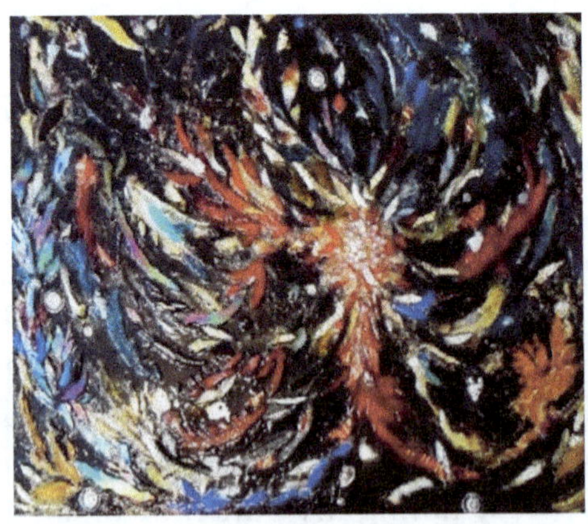

My gratitude is limitless. For my readers, I wish for you to know how unique you are and that all is provided.

Enjoy your lives, there has only been one of you, there is only one of you, there will never be another. You are unique.

Blessings to you always, all ways. Love, from Eleanor Ruth Fisher.